THE WITCH'S COMPLETE GUIDE TO TAROT

chartwell
books

Brimming with creative inspiration, how-to projects, and useful information to enrich your everyday life, www.Quarto.com is a favorite destination for those pursuing their interests and passions. Visit our site and dig deeper with our books into your area of interest: Quarto Creates, Quarto Cooks, Quarto Homes, Quarto Lives, Quarto Drives, Quarto Explores, Quarto Gifts, or Quarto Kids.

This edition published in 2022 by Chartwell Books,
an imprint of The Quarto Group
142 West 36th Street, 4th Floor
New York, NY 10018 USA

T (212) 779-4972 F (212) 779-6058
www.Quarto.com

10 9 8 7 6 5 4 3 2 1

Chartwell titles are also available at discount for retail, wholesale, promotional, and bulk purchase. For details, contact the Special Sales Manager by email at specialsales@quarto.com or by mail at The Quarto Group, Attn: Special Sales Manager, 100 Cummings Center Suite 265D, Beverly, MA 01915, USA.

ISBN: 978-0-7858-4079-4

Library of Congress Control Number: 2022931183

Publisher: Wendy Friedman
Editorial Director: Betina Cochran
Creative Director: Pauline Molinari
Editor: Meredith Mennitt
Designer: Erin Fahringer

Image credits: Shutterstock

Printed in China

THE WITCH'S Complete Guide TO TAROT

Unlock Your Intuition and Discover the Power of Tarot

Patti Wigington

chartwell
books

CONTENTS

INTRODUCTION

Cross my palm with silver, and I will tell you of your destiny.

How many times have you seen that old chestnut in a movie or television show where a character is getting a Tarot reading? It's usually uttered in some vaguely Eastern European-ish accent by an actress who is either old and wizened, or young and super-sultry. She typically murmurs something like I see a long journey, a handsome stranger . . . and then she flips over the Death card, and all hell breaks loose. Of course, this is because if movies portrayed Tarot readings accurately, they'd be, frankly, far less dramatic.

Contrary to what we see in pop culture, reading Tarot cards has nothing to do with "seeing the future." It's not "fortune-telling," in the classic sense of the word, although it's certainly a method of divination. Instead, Tarot is a tool for self-evaluation, an opportunity for insight into where we've been, where we are, and where we're likely to go. But just like so many other aspects of life, where we're headed can change. Nothing is etched in stone, and if we don't like what we see as a potential outcome, we can make things unfold differently simply by making different choices.

I've been a practicing witch and Tarot reader for more than half my life. I got my first deck of Tarot cards in 1987, when I was eighteen, so you can do the math. It's been a minute. Although I had no idea how to get started, I diligently studied the little white book that came with the deck, read several books on Tarot, and dove into it.

Honestly, it was a disaster. The first reading I did for myself took over two hours—I used the Celtic Cross layout, which is a fairly complicated spread and was probably a terrible choice for a newbie. I spent an innumerable amount of time looking up definitions for each card, writing it down in painful detail . . . and didn't learn a damn thing. After a while, I put the cards back in their neat little box, where they sat, undisturbed for several weeks.

As the years went on, I figured out that I didn't need to do a massive Tarot spread every time I had a simple question. In fact, I learned if I simply pulled one card each day, I could familiarize myself with the deck while also gaining a better understanding of how the morning's card related to things that happened later on in the day. And then, after a decade or so, I stopped opening the little white books and looking up individual meanings, and I just trusted my gut and began to read the cards intuitively.

That was when it finally clicked for me. I'd figured out the secret that none of the books had told me: that what a card means for one person isn't the same as what it means for the next person . . . because we're all different. My Seven of Wands is different from someone else's Seven of Wands. Sure, the symbolism is essentially the same, but what it means and how it's relevant is completely unique for each of us.

Once I learned to follow my instincts as a reader, it wasn't a big leap to start incorporating my Tarot practice into my work with magic and witchcraft. A quick disclaimer here—while many witches do read Tarot, the art of Tarot reading is not a uniquely witchy activity. There are plenty of Tarot readers—quite good ones—who are not witches. Many are Christian, and plenty follow other religious traditions (or none at all). Reading Tarot doesn't make you a witch. It makes you a Tarot reader.

All of that said, I've learned (through a lot of trial and error) that if we can understand Tarot as a tool for self-evaluation and introspection, we can also view it as a mechanism for self-development and personal growth. We can adapt its symbolism—no matter which deck we're using—into spellwork, ritual, and magic in a way that allows us to embrace our authentic selves, celebrate who we are and who we wish to become, and indulge in transformative self-empowerment. Tarot cards and all of the included icons, archetypes, and hidden mysteries can be included in our spellwork and ritual just as we would include any other ingredient, like crystals, herbs, or oils.

This book is a bit different than your standard Tarot books—after all, there are only so many ways people can describe what the Five of Coins means when it appears. Although we'll talk in part 2 about the meanings of the cards (because you do need to know them), what we're going to focus on instead is how you can incorporate the power of Tarot into your practice of magic. Through ritual, spellwork, and other action items, you'll unlock the keys to some doors you may not have realized were even locked.

Opening those doors might be uncomfortable on occasion. It might even make you feel vulnerable or scared. But as Brené Brown says in her groundbreaking book Daring Greatly, it is only the person who is vulnerable who allows themselves to live wholeheartedly. It's the individual willing to bare their soul who can exist in a way that's authentic and free of artifice.

That can be some pretty heady stuff. Are you ready to join me on this journey?

Let's talk Tarot.

1

WHY READ TAROT?

Not too long ago, I was at an event that had hired me to provide readings for their evening's entertainment. I'd been booked to read Tarot cards for party guests for three hours straight. Each guest had a ten-minute time limit, and by the time I'd worked with the first four or five attendees, people were literally standing in a line outside the room in which I was reading, ignoring the delicious buffet spread and board games the hostess had put out for them. Everyone wanted a reading.

At one point in the evening, I finished a reading and asked the guest if he had any additional questions. He did. He asked me why I read Tarot cards. He wasn't asking why I was there, that night, reading cards—the answer was obvious: I was being paid very well. But he wanted to know why I read them at all.

The answer was a fairly straightforward one: because they help us to sort through things that we might not otherwise be able to.

The best analogy I can give is one of those "choose your own adventure" books that were so popular when I was an adolescent. I remember reading those, making complicated decisions at the end of each page. If I wanted to open the spooky door to the hallway, I turned to page 23. But if I thought it was better to go outside and smell some flowers, that was page 117.

And then when I got to page 117, smelled some pretty flowers, and then fell into a hidden pit of quicksand, never to be seen again, I went back to the last page and opened the spooky door instead.

That's a bit like reading Tarot. If I turn over a card that says I have a choice between the spooky hallway and the flowers in the garden, and I don't like what's lurking beyond the magnolias, well, I can make different decisions.

When we read Tarot, we get a chance to allow our subconscious to explore our options for us. We can use it to answer open-ended questions. Clients sometimes ask me things like, "When will my boyfriend move back in with me?" or "What company will I have my next job with?" and there's no clear answer for something like that. But if they ask, "What needs to happen for me to salvage this broken relationship?" or "How can I find career satisfaction?" that's a whole different ballgame.

Although Tarot readers aren't therapists, they often find themselves helping clients talk through a situation objectively. I've always said that the cards don't usually reveal surprises. Instead, they validate what you already knew and may not have wanted to accept or understand. By taking the time to look at what the cards are saying to us, and how they apply to the individual asking the questions, we can guide ourselves through many of life's uncertainties, and make decisions appropriately.

I've learned that by asking the cards questions and mindfully evaluating what they reveal, I can gain insight into past influences, my current situation, and how things are likely to unfold if I continue on my current trajectory. Do I open the spooky door or go out in the garden with the flowers?

Before we go any further, here's a quick disclaimer: if you're struggling with medical or mental health issues, seek professional care. While Tarot can be a helpful addition to your life, it's no substitute for the services of a qualified, trained health-care professional. Don't be embarrassed to ask for help; reach out for the proper assistance if and when you need it. Your Tarot cards will still be waiting when you're ready to read them.

2
THE BASICS OF TAROT

Before we take a really deep dive into working with Tarot cards, let's go over some of the basics. If you've read Tarot before, much of this will seem familiar—consider this chapter a refresher. On the other hand, if you're new to the world of Tarot, this is a very bare-bones outline of how the cards work and what you can learn from them. At the end of this book in the Resources section, you'll find a comprehensive list that includes many of my favorite books on Tarot. Add some of these to your reading list to learn all about the subtle nuances of this vibrant and exciting divination method.

To those who are unfamiliar with various forms of divination—not just Tarot, but everything else, like pendulum work, astrology, scrying, and so on—reading the cards has an air of the unknown about the process. It all seems very ethereal and mystical, doesn't

it? However, you don't have to be some sort of grand and powerful psychic to work with Tarot cards. With some practice and patience, you can learn to read the cards too. I always tell people that while Tarot isn't for everyone, it can be for anyone.

A Tarot deck includes a total of seventy-eight cards. The first twenty-two, known as the Major Arcana, are cards with heavily symbolic meanings that focus on various aspects of our existence. Primarily, they represent our spiritual journey, the intuitive mind, and the many realms of ongoing change. These cards are numbered, beginning with the Fool (0) who represents someone at the beginning stages of their development, and ending with the

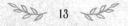

World (21), which is associated with completion. We'll get into more detail on the specifics of each card in part 2.

In addition to the Major Arcana, there are fifty-six cards comprised of the four suits: Cups, Swords, Wands, and Pentacles (or Coins). Cup cards represent our interpersonal relationships and various aspects of our emotions. Conflict, challenges, and even moral issues can appear in the suit of Swords. The Wands symbolize things like communication, jobs and career matters, our education, and forward activity. Finally, the Pentacles—which instead appear as Coins in some decks—focus on the material aspects of our lives, such as money, security, and stability.

Typically, a reader will turn over cards in a predetermined pattern, called a layout or spread, with each position in the spread representing a specific facet of the overall reading. For instance, the first card might represent the past, while the last indicates the future. A card in the center could be associated with the present situation, while all the cards surrounding it show what sorts of things or people have the most influence on the question at hand. The number of spreads available to you is limitless, and many readers make up their own spreads. In chapter 12, I'll share with you some simple yet effective layouts you can use for different purposes. If you feel like you don't connect with them, that's totally fine—try creating one that's as unique as you are!

In addition to using Tarot for divination, many people in the magical community use the cards as tools or ingredients in spellwork and rituals. We will get into that in part 3, where you will learn why and how to incorporate Tarot into magic. But to get the most out of that sort of practice, it's important to understand (and possibly unlearn) some of the things you may have heard or read about Tarot already.

Myths And Misconceptions

We've already discussed that Tarot cards don't predict the future—they simply help us evaluate what might be coming around the next bend. Yet there is still an idea that Tarot is some spooky occult mystery practice that only Very Powerful Witches can do, and that's simply not the case. Let's break down some of the most popular myths and misconceptions about Tarot. I'm about to drop some truth bombs here, so buckle up.

MYTH: *You have to be a witch, or at the very least a psychic, to successfully read Tarot.*

FACT: One of the greatest things about Tarot is any person who's motivated to study and practice can read the cards. Many highly successful readers are not witches and don't consider themselves psychics; however, they'd probably tell you what makes them good at what they do is learning to trust their intuition.

Everyone has some degree of intuition; the problem is, most people are told their entire lives not to listen to that quiet inner voice. How many times have you thought something was true—you just knew it—but you didn't go with your gut because you'd convinced yourself (or someone else had convinced you) it was all in your head? Yes, that inner voice. If you're willing to learn something new, follow your intuition, and develop your skills, then Tarot reading might just be for you—witch or not. And who knows? Once you start using Tarot cards for magic, you might even decide to explore witchcraft itself on a deeper level.

MYTH: *Reading Tarot can be dangerous/evil/bad.*

FACT: In some religions, any form of divination is frowned upon. I'm not here to tell anyone that their religious belief is right or wrong. But what I can and will tell you is this: Tarot card artwork is a collection of symbols and archetypes. To say that these images are "dangerous" is as silly as saying an ink blob on a Rorschach test is evil because someone looked at it and saw something that horrified them (never mind the fact the next person saw cute kittens or fluffy baby rabbits in the very same spatter of ink). These images and archetypes represent the many aspects of human existence, both on the material and spiritual planes. For some people, that's frightening because we don't always want to acknowledge the truth or reality of our situation. That doesn't make Tarot dangerous; it just makes it scary because as humans, we sometimes dislike things we don't understand.

MYTH: *You should never buy your own Tarot cards; only use cards that you receive as a gift.*

FACT: No one knows exactly where this legend started, but most readers will tell you it's patently false. I've got dozens of Tarot decks that I've purchased for myself because they spoke to me, or I thought the artwork was pretty, or there was something about them that I just liked. If I waited around for someone to give me a deck, I'd never have gotten around to reading cards at all.

In fact, you probably should pick out your own deck. It's the difference between working with a set of cards that you love and one that you're sort of ambivalent about because someone got you something that didn't really excite you. Do you rely on other people to know what you want and what speaks to you about other aspects of your life? Pick your own cards and enjoy them! We'll talk more in chapter 4 about how to select a deck that really speaks to you, as well as tips to follow for making your own set if you're feeling super motivated!

MYTH: *Reversed cards mean the opposite, so they're negative.*

FACT: This is a common misconception, and honestly, I can't fault people for thinking this. Many of the Tarot guidebooks attribute concepts like despair or tragedy or deceit to reversed cards.

In most parts of our lives, when we see something upside down, it's the direct opposite of what it is when it appears upright. With Tarot, it's slightly different.

Think of the Tarot cards and their meanings as appearing on a spectrum. Some mean sunshine and joy, others mean catastrophe and sadness, but there's a whole wide world of variation between those two points. Each card has multiple possible interpretations depending on the situation. If we look at that spectrum as ranging from shadow to light, then maybe that reversed card could indicate you need to look at the shadow aspects of the meanings. We'll talk more about shadow work in part 3.

MYTH: *You should never read your own Tarot cards.*

FACT: When my car breaks down, I take it to my mechanic. When my mechanic's car breaks down, he fixes it himself. Why? Because he can! He's got the skills, the know-how, the tools, and the experience. He's not going to take it to some other mechanic. There's no rule that mechanics shouldn't fix their own cars. Likewise, it's okay to read your own cards when you need some insight.

There's a myth that reading your own cards will bring great misfortune, and that's simply untrue. That said, there are times when you should probably ask for someone else's assistance. If you're reading your cards and feel as though you can't be objective—maybe you just keep on flipping cards around until you get the answer you want to see—then it's time to ask a trusted friend or an ethical professional for a second opinion. But for everyday problem solving and resolution of issues on which you can be fair and unbiased toward yourself? Go ahead and read them!

MYTH: *Tarot cards are never wrong.*

FACT: Our futures depend on a lot of things. Possible outcomes are always changeable, and they can be impacted by the decisions and choices we make. While the cards may paint a picture of a future you don't like, nothing is etched in stone. Their answers are based upon where things stand for us in the here and now. Want a different outcome? Make a different choice. Turn left instead of right. Stay instead of go. Speak instead of remaining silent. You'll change your own destiny, and the cards will guide you on that journey.

3

A Brief History of Tarot

Although divination in its many forms has been documented
back to the earliest parts of mankind's recorded history, the use
of Tarot cards is comparatively new. In fact, they started out as a
fun party game for rich Italians and French aristocrats just a few
centuries ago. Let's explore some of the history and look at how
and why this lighthearted after-dinner entertainment turned into
a magical tool filled with divinatory symbolism and imagery.

European Parlor Games

In the late fourteenth century, wealthy European families discovered card games, and one of the most popular was called tarocchini or tarocchi in Italy and jeu de tarot in France. It was a big hit at parties—sort of like our grandparents getting together for bridge night—and variations emerged throughout the period. One game involved taking tricks from other players, similar to a round of whist, and in another version, players were dealt random cards from which they had to compose poems based upon the pictures. Whoever's poetry was judged to be the best was the winner of the game. As you can imagine, it was pretty good entertainment when one was sitting around listening to an orchestra or waiting for a duel to liven things up. Most of these early cards contained only pips, or numbered cards, with no court cards like knights, queens, or kings.

However, that all changed thanks to people like Filippo Visconti, the Duke of Milan, who thought if playing card games with numbers was fun, it could be even more exciting to play with cards that had pictures of his family on them. Visconti and his son-in-law, Francesco Sforza, invited artist Bonifacio Bembo to paint portraits of various family members, creating a series of court cards to add to the pips. Sforza's wife, Bianca Maria Visconti, appeared as the Popess, seated upon a golden throne while holding a staff adorned with a cross. Visconti's other family members appeared as assorted figures throughout the hand-painted cards, and several decks were created for the Viscontis. Partial collections of these decks can still be seen in museum collections today.

Soon enough, the trend exploded, and the upper-class friends of the Visconti-Sforzas all wanted their own personalized card decks too. Because the printing press hadn't really taken off yet, customized cards with family portraits were a novelty only the very rich could afford; after all, they essentially had to hire someone to paint a dozen or so very tiny portraits.

By the fifteenth century, a German goldsmith named Johannes Gutenberg had invented a way to automate the printing process. Although he wasn't the first to use woodblock printing (that was done in China at least six centuries earlier) or moveable metal type (which Korean bookmakers were already using), Gutenberg's new printing press used a screw to mash down the inked metal typeface, creating a fast, efficient, and inexpensive way to print books, broadsheets, and pamphlets. Naturally, playing cards followed along quickly, and soon, even the average family could have a deck of cards in their home to play jeu de tarot

by candlelight after dinner. Suddenly, card games became a pastime that was for everyone, not just the wealthy. Of course, people also found other ways to amuse themselves with cards, and it's estimated that using playing cards for divination began to take hold around the late sixteenth and early seventeenth centuries.

By the time another century or so had passed, people were beginning to assign specific meanings to the cards that had previously just been part of a simple parlor game and even creating precise methods in which the cards could be laid out for divination. In the late eighteenth century, Antoine Court de Gébelin, a French Freemason and former Protestant minister, published a book declaring Tarot held secret meanings based on ancient esoteric practices rooted in Egypt. Printers caught on to this, and Tarot decks were soon being published with court card images that contained symbolism directly based upon de Gébelin's analysis, despite there being no actual historical evidence to support de Gébelin's claims.

A few years later, French occultist Jean-Baptiste Alliette released a treatise of his own, explaining how people could use the Tarot for in-depth divination. In 1791, he published the first Tarot deck designed specifically for divinatory purposes.

The Spiritualist Movement and Divination

Interest in divination, mysticism, and the occult continued to grow, and by the Victorian era, Tarot reading, seances, and spiritualism were popular pastimes for bored upper-class families. Beginning around 1850, the spiritualist movement became a trend in both England and the United States, and topics like mesmerism, thought-reading, and clairvoyance all evolved into popular subjects for dinnertime conversation.

The movement included an influx of people who made a good deal of money by claiming to be mediums who could speak to the dead. When word got out that Queen Victoria and her husband, Prince Albert, had attended seances, an entire subculture bloomed featuring mediums, paranormal researchers, ghost-hunting clubs, automatic writing, spiritualist newsletters, and more. Naturally, divination in a variety of forms also saw a rise in popularity.

As spiritualism swept nineteenth-century England, numerous occult societies began to emerge from the shadows, including the Hermetic Order of the Golden Dawn, which founded its first temple in London in the late 1880s. Early members included the noted occultist Aleister Crowley, Irish poet and dramatist William Butler Yeats, and esoteric author Arthur Edward Waite. In 1909, Waite commissioned the deck that has since become the gold standard: Rider Waite Smith.

The Legacy of Pamela Colman Smith

When Arthur Waite visited the British Museum and saw images of a full deck of Tarot cards known as the Sola Busca, he was immediately inspired. First created in 1490, the Sola Busca is the earliest complete Tarot deck in existence today and is the only one known to include illustrations on all of the pip cards rather than merely numbered dots. Waite decided to craft a deck of his own, heavily influenced by Kabbalistic symbolism, but he wasn't an artist. Enter Pamela Colman Smith.

Smith, known to her friends as Pixie, was a London-born artist who spent her childhood traveling back and forth between Manchester and Jamaica with her parents. Writings by her contemporaries, as well as her own private artwork and correspondences, suggest she was likely biracial (of African and European heritage) and had several romantic relationships with women. She lived a free-spirited, bohemian lifestyle, traveling the world and surrounding herself with art and artists.

In addition to writing books of her own, including an illustrated collection of Jamaican folk tales, Smith provided art for several works by other authors like Bram Stoker and Yeats. In 1901, she joined the Golden Dawn, and when the group disbanded, Waite approached her with his Tarot idea. Smith used the Sola Busca artwork for inspiration and was the first contemporary artist to use characters as representative images in the lower cards. Instead of showing merely a cluster of cups, coins, wands, or swords, Smith incorporated human figures into the artwork, and the result is the iconic deck that every reader knows today. It sold for six shillings when it was released.

Smith received no royalties from the sale of the deck and died penniless in Cornwall in 1951, but her work has been reprinted millions of times over. Although the artwork may appear simple on the surface, its deceptive complexity makes the Rider-Waite-Smith deck a valuable tool for intuitive readers. Many of us owe a great debt to Pamela Colman Smith for providing us with a collection of seventy-eight paintings that delve so deeply into our minds and hearts.

4
CHOOSING YOUR DECK

For anyone new to the world of Tarot—or even, for that matter, those of us who have been at it for a while—choosing a deck of cards can be an intimidating process. In addition to the dozens of variations of Rider Waite Smith, there are thousands of other collections out there. There are decks based on movies and television series, mythology from around the world, fantasy art and classical paintings, vampires, zombies, cats, dogs, and even baseball. Whatever you're interested in, there's probably a Tarot deck for it! Honestly, the very act of selecting can be overwhelming if you aren't sure where to begin.

Many people opt to start with a version of Rider Waite Smith. It's the one most often used for imagery in books on how to read Tarot, so if you're someone who needs that visual connection, it makes perfectly good sense to do this. For this very reason, it's not a bad choice for beginners. On the other hand, if you just don't feel any affinity at all for the artwork in the Rider-Waite-Smith decks, then you're going to have to do a little bit of work. Plenty of Tarot readers will tell you they chose a deck that "spoke to them," or "just felt right." But how do you get to where a deck speaks to you, or makes you feel anything at all?

Your first step is to handle a variety of Tarot decks. If you've got friends who are

Meditation Ritual to Help Select Your Deck

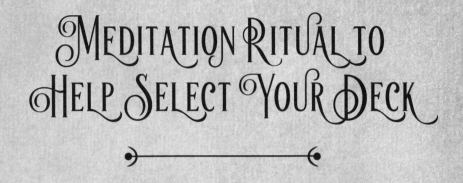

———— ⚬———⚬ ————

This simple meditation ritual is one you can do right before you go shopping for cards. By intuitively preparing yourself in advance, you'll be far better positioned to identify which Tarot deck speaks to you best, and fits your style, so you can give it a forever home.

Find a place where you can work alone and uninterrupted. If you'd like to light your favorite incense or a candle, go ahead! Put on some ambient music if you want or some nature sounds in the background. If you can do this ritual outside, even better!

Sit quietly and close your eyes. Breathe slowly and deeply, inhaling and exhaling. Become acutely aware of your surroundings. What scents are in the air around you? What sounds do you hear off in the distance? What does the floor–or ground, if you're outside–feel like beneath you? Immerse yourself completely in your environment, continuing to regulate your breath.

Visualize yourself walking through a natural setting–what appeals to you the most? Are you in the woods? On a windy mountaintop? Perhaps you're wandering along a shoreline. Imagine yourself walking calmly, quietly, along a path through this world. The path meanders and dips, crossing over peaks and valleys, and although you can't see precisely what's ahead, you know there is no danger. You are calm and at peace as you make your journey.

Ahead of you, in the distance, visualize a soft, glowing light. As you move closer, you realize the light is welcoming, full of positive and inspiring energy. Continue walking toward it, knowing nothing there will harm you. When you reach the light, look deep inside it to reveal the source.

In the center of the light, you'll see a deck of cards. They may be vague in appearance, or they may be very specific. Perhaps their images are just a blur to you–that's okay. Reach out and touch them. Hold them, exploring their vibration and energy. How do they make you feel as you hold them in your hands? Take as much time as you need so you'll remember the sensation of the cards–not just their physical attributes, but the way you respond to them intuitively, spiritually, and emotionally.

When you're ready, return the cards to their spot inside the glowing light, and begin making your journey back. Visualize yourself walking back to your starting point, always remembering the feel of the cards in your hands. Once you've gotten back to where you began, take a few moments to breathe, and gradually allow yourself to return to a state of clarity.

When you're ready, go out and look for cards at your favorite local shop. Touch them, handle them, feel them beneath your fingertips, and when you find the deck that matches the sensation of the one in your visualization journey, you'll know that's the deck for you.

interested in Tarot, ask them which decks they prefer. Be sure to ask why they like them. Additionally, you may want to visit a local metaphysical shop to see what options are out there. Certainly, you could go to a large chain bookstore, but a smaller, local shop will often have loose cards lying around. Publishers sometimes send sample cards for marketing purposes so customers can see what's actually inside the package. While you probably won't get to see every single card in the deck, you should see enough of them to give you an idea if you like it or not.

It's important to note there are many cards on the market that are created for divinatory purposes but are not true Tarot decks. You may see some presented as oracle decks, wisdom cards, affirmation cards, or some variation thereof. While these are great tools to use for divination, they're not the same as a Tarot deck. Make sure you're purchasing a set that has the traditional seventy-eight cards.

As you're looking at the various decks of cards, pay attention to see if there's one that stands out to you more than others. Is there an Art Deco set you find aesthetically pleasing? Do you absolutely love that Golden Girls Tarot collection because it reminds you of all those nights you spent bingeing the series with your Nana before she passed away? Maybe you love one of the many dog or cat Tarot decks because volunteering for an animal rescue is your passion.

Look at and handle as many decks as you can—and don't settle for something you don't feel a connection to. When the right one appears, you'll know.

Can I Make My Own Cards?

If you're a crafty, creative sort, and you'd like to make your own Tarot cards, great! No rule says you can only use commercially manufactured ones. All Tarot decks began in someone's imagination, so why not yours? Making a deck of your own is a great way to express your interests creatively while also meeting your spiritual needs. In many traditions of witchcraft, any act of creation is a magical process in and of itself, so if you're willing to put time, energy, and effort into it, you should absolutely do so!

There are several different ways to do this, and you should choose the one that works best for you. First, you may want to consider buying a set of blanks, a deck of seventy-eight unprinted, plain Tarot-sized cards. You can create any artwork you like on them. Another option—and certainly the most affordable—is to use cardstock and cut them out yourself. Neither method is superior to the other; do what works best with your skills and resources.

Do you draw or paint? Do you create digital artwork with your tablet or laptop? Maybe you're a mixed-media artist. Some people make their own Tarot decks with images they've found online and printed out. Keep in mind that images on the internet are often copyrighted, so if you print and use them for personal use, you may be allowed to do so, but it would be illegal to reproduce them for commercial use. If you're not sure if an image can be legally copied for personal use, check with the creator. Many talented artists have made their own Tarot designs available for free to anyone for personal projects.

Take some time to think about the different types of symbolism you want to incorporate into your deck. Perhaps you're a mechanic—maybe you'd like to use wrenches for Wands, or lug nuts for Coins. If your passion is cooking, think about using pots or pans for your suit of Cups, and chef's knives for your Sword cards. Maybe you'd like to create a deck based upon your favorite movie or television series, or the plants in your garden, or your kids' drawings from school. The sky is the limit when you're creating your own Tarot deck.

Whatever your method, take plenty of time to create a custom deck that meets your own needs and wants, and it will be as unique as you are.

5

PROTECTING YOUR CARDS

After all that searching, you've finally found your deck! Congratulations! Now that you've done so, though, it's a good idea to protect your cards when you're not using them. With some basic protection techniques, you can keep your cards safe from both physical damage and from negative energy. Consider ritually consecrating your deck, and then storing the cards in a small box or bag, or even wrapped in a scarf. Ideally, you shouldn't just leave your Tarot cards scattered all willy-nilly around the place. Between uses, you don't necessarily have to leave your cards wrapped in silk and kept somewhere sacred, but many people feel this can help them develop a better connection to their cards. Treat your Tarot deck like the sacred and magical tool it is, and you'll find you can have a better relationship with your cards.

When you first get a new deck of cards, take some time to "get to know the deck" before you use them the first time. Some people like to put them under their pillow for a few nights so the cards can acquire their personal energy, but you don't necessarily have to do

this. Realistically, having a brick of Tarot cards under your head as you sleep may be impractical. Instead, you can carry your cards with you as you go about your daily business, place them on your magical altar, or even store them with a quartz crystal that has absorbed your personal energy.

Many Tarot readers never allow anyone else to touch their deck of cards because the cards tend to pick up on the vibrations around them. Imagine if you had a friend come over when they felt grumpy or sad, and then they handled your cards. How would your deck feel to you after that? If it's been a while since you've picked up your deck, or if they've been handled by someone whose presence bothers you, either ritually reconsecrate them or carry them with you for a while until they "feel right" again.

Crafting Your Own Storage Box or Bag

While you can certainly keep your cards in the original packaging–especially if you love the artwork–you may want to make each set their very own bag or box for storage. The magical act of creation can help you feel more connected to the energy of your Tarot cards. You can sew a simple bag or decorate a box with supplies you probably have lying around the house.

To make a basic drawstring bag, you'll need a rectangular piece of fabric about 14-inch long by 6-inch wide, as well as two 12-inch lengths of ribbon and a handful of beads, which should have holes large enough for you to run the ribbon through. Although this is a simple project with a sewing machine, if you don't have one, no worries. This is easy enough to sew by hand with a needle and thread.

Before you cut anything, fold your fabric in half and lay your Tarot deck on top of it to make sure you've got enough material—you don't want to cut and sew your bag only to discover it's too small! On each of the short ends of the fabric, use an iron to press down about an inch of material, and then fold the raw edge under toward the wrong side. Stitch this with a seam allowance of about ⅝ inches to create the channel for your drawstrings.

Next, fold the material in half, right sides together, matching up the drawstring channels on the short ends and the outer edges. Stitch the two long sides from the fold line to the stitches you made in the first step. This creates the bag shape with a pair of channels at the top that remains open at each end. Now, turn the bag right side out.

Use a safety pin to thread the ribbons through the channels, starting on one side of the bag, looping around on the opposite side, and then ending back where you began. This will give you two ribbons that cross over each other. Knot the beads on the end of the ribbons and tie the ends together. By pulling on the beads on each side, you'll easily be able to cinch the bag closed.

If you knit or crochet, you can make your own bag with yarn and your favorite pattern; a typical Tarot bag measures about 6 to 8 inches tall and 4 to 6 inches wide. Whatever size you choose to make, be sure it will fit your deck of cards comfortably. Too big, and your cards will slide around and possibly become bent or damaged; too small, and you'll have to force them into the bag.

Some people aren't handy with a sewing machine or needle arts, and if that's you, that'! Try wrapping your cards in a simple square of cloth, pulling it snug, and tying it closed with a ribbon or extra piece of fabric. You can use a bandanna or scarf for this, and it doesn't have to be silk unless that's what you like.

If you prefer something a little more solid and secure, decorate a simple box instead and use that to protect your cards. Start by picking up a plain box either of wood, tin, or anything else you like. Here are some ways you can personalize it and make it uniquely, magically yours:

Sand a wooden box, draw a design in pencil, and then use a woodburning tool to make the image permanent. Once it's complete, seal the wood with a thin layer of clear coat or oil to protect it.

Cut out images of artwork you love or pieces of decorative patterned paper, and decoupage them onto the outside of your box.

Find a box with a photo frame in the lid and use it to display a sample copy of one of the cards in your deck, an image of the god or goddess of your tradition, an ancestor you may be working with, or any other sort of artwork that speaks to you.

Cover a box with a base layer of acrylic paint, and then decorate it with magical sigils and symbols.

Finally, don't forget that one of the hallmarks of being an effective magic practitioner is the ability to make magic with what's readily available to you. If you don't have fabric, sewing supplies, or even an empty box nearby, what can you use instead? There are plenty of containers or vessels that lend themselves well to Tarot storage; I've used zippered cosmetic pouches, coin purses with snap closures, and even an old tobacco tin. Once you've found the right box or bag for your cards, be sure to cleanse it before placing your deck inside it, particularly if you're repurposing a pre-loved item. You can do a simple elemental cleansing at your magical workspace by passing the bag or box over representations of the four classical elements: earth, air, fire, and water. If you prefer, leave your container out under the full moon overnight, or burn purifying herbs and pass the box or bag through the smoke; some of my favorites for this method are rosemary, mugwort, lavender, mint, and bay leaves. Alternatively, you can include your new box or bag in a ritual to cleanse the deck itself.

Simple Card Cleansing Ritual

Some people cleanse their cards every time they use them; some do it randomly. When should you do it? Any time you feel your cards need it! If you don't believe cards acquire and retain energy from those who have touched them in the past, feel free to skip this section.

Many people in the magical community believe material items carry the vibrations of people who have been in contact with them. This means if you don't cleanse the residual energy from an item you've brought home for magical work like spells, divination, or rituals, you could inadvertently pick up on someone else's energy, for better or for worse. Now, with a new item, such as a deck fresh out of its shrink-wrap, there may not be much clinging to it, but it's a good idea to cleanse it anyway because who knows what sorts of things (or people) it came into contact with before it got to you?

There's no one right way to cleanse magical items, so if you already have a cleansing or purification ritual that works for you, you don't have to stop using it! This simple ritual is one you can use to cleanse your Tarot deck, but it can be adapted for any other magical item—talismans and amulets, wands and athames, candles and crystals, and so on—that needs cleansing. If you need to tweak any of this to meet your own needs, go ahead!

In addition to your Tarot deck, you'll need a white candle, a bowl of soil, your favorite incense, a small tealight, and a cup of water. If you're part of a magical tradition that casts a circle before a ritual, go ahead and do so, but it's not necessary. To begin, place the bowl of

* Wash your hands before using them; oils from your skin can eventually damage the ink and paper on your cards, so clean hands will help your cards last longer.
* Lay them on a clean surface when you're doing a reading or creating spellwork or ritual with them.
* Once you're done using your cards for a reading or in a spell, return them to their box or bag. If they've managed to acquire dust, clean them before you put them away. Usually, a simple swipe with a dry cloth will remove any dust. If your cards feel sticky or tacky, wipe them down with a slightly damp soft cloth over the flat surfaces only, avoiding the edges.
* Keep your cards away from curious pets, exploring children, open flames, sticky food, and spillable beverages.

soil in the northernmost part of your altar, the incense to the east, the tealight in the south, and the water to the west. Light the white candle, and say, Power of light, power of purity, by this sacred flame, I cleanse these cards.

Pass the cards over the bowl of soil, representing the element of earth. Say, Guardians of the North, powers of the earth, I call upon you to cleanse these cards, providing your stable, secure, and grounding energies. Light the incense, and pass your Tarot deck through the smoke, saying, Guardians of the East, powers of air, I call upon you to cleanse these cards, providing the gifts of wisdom, intuition, and clear communication. Move to the tealight candle and light it, passing the cards over the flame—but not too close! Say, Guardians of the South, powers of fire, I call upon you to cleanse these cards, providing passion, power, and the strength of my will. Finally, pass the cards over the cup of water, saying, Guardians of the West, powers of water, I call upon you to cleanse these cards, providing your cleansing, purifying, healing energies.

Focus on the light from the white candle, allowing that light to surround your cards. Know without a doubt that your cards are absorbing the positive energy from the candle and from the four elements. Say, I cleanse these cards by the powers of earth, of air, of fire, and of water. I banish the energies of any previous owners, of any who came before me, and make these cards new and fresh. I cleanse these cards with the powers and energies of the elements, and they are now mine.

Remember that in addition to regularly performing metaphysical actions such as a cleansing ritual—if you think your cards need it— there are a few mundane, or non-magical, actions you should take to keep your cards physically clean:

6

The Major Arcana

Some of the Tarot's most iconic artwork comes to us from Pamela Colman Smith's paintings in the Major Arcana. You've probably seen these cards before—Death, the Fool, the Hermit, and so on. Within the Major Arcana, you'll find three different groups of cards, each representing various realms of human experience. These three different areas, or themes, are of the material world, the intuitive mind, and overall change.

The first set, the cards numbered 0–7, generally represent matters of the material world, situations related to jobs and career success, financial gain or loss, education, and marriage or other romantic partnerships. The second group, cards 8–14, focus on our individual, emotional selves. Rather than addressing what we do or think, they center around how we feel. This group symbolizes the deeply human need for emotional connection with others, as well as our search for faith and truth. Finally, cards 15–21 show us the way to enlightenment, dealing with universal laws and issues. These cards are more about the many different aspects of our lives related to spiritual growth and development and focus less on the feelings of the individual or societal needs.

0 THE FOOL

The Fool is many things, but he's not foolish. Think of the Fool as representing the earliest phases of spiritual development. In general, the Fool is a symbol of not only new beginnings but also inexperience. The Fool isn't especially rational or sensible at all, but that doesn't matter; it's time for new adventures and journeys, and all of the unknown possibilities that lie on the road ahead. Everything has potential, and there may be a need to improvise as the road twists and turns. Be spontaneous, but also mindful of your steps.

When appearing reversed, the Fool can indicate someone with a tendency to not "look before they leap" and serves as a reminder to think before we act. Additionally, it cautions us that a lack of attention to detail can be problematic later, causing us to make mistakes. Don't let your fears of the unknown hold you back.

1 THE MAGICIAN

The Magician is a card of opportunity. When it pops up in a Tarot reading, consider it a sign that with the right direction, you have the power to manifest your intentions, but some hard work will be required. The Magician reminds us we can be the masters of our own destiny and bring about the changes we wish to see, by sheer force of will and action. Through self-awareness of our vision and goal, deliberate choices, and conscious activity, we can make big things happen.

If the Magician shows up reversed, it can indicate weakness and ineptitude. This could represent a person who fails not because they make poor decisions, but because they make no decisions at all. Get focused, get clear, and get moving.

2 THE HIGH PRIESTESS

Think of the High Priestess as the bridge between that which we can see and the world of the unknown. This card presents both balance and power in one form and often represents an unrevealed future with hidden influences at work. Although the High Priestess is a feminine-presenting figure, the card doesn't necessarily represent a woman. Instead, it's a reminder of the feminine-assigned attributes we all carry within us, such as wisdom, enlightenment, and intuition. The High Priestess is a card associated with creative personalities— poets, musicians, and artists, for instance—and is truly a card of manifestation, often possible because of our connection to our higher selves.

In reverse, the High Priestess card can symbolize open knowledge and obvious facts that you've been ignoring. Not only that, but you're also probably denying your intuitive hunches in a way that's rooted in pride and conceit. Learn to occasionally slow down, calm your breath, and listen to what the universe is trying to tell you.

3 THE EMPRESS

When the Empress appears in your Tarot spread, look for material bounty and richness in addition to fertility—and this isn't automatically the fertility regarding children. Instead, it's the fertility of abundance for anyone who is trying to manifest contentment, love, or creative endeavors. What do you wish to bring into your life that's new and satisfying? If this card appears, it can sometimes represent a sense of pleasure in all the things you already have, and not just what you wish to achieve. Particularly when it comes to family and home life, the Empress is a card of harmony, a nurturing Earth Mother archetype.

As you might imagine, in reverse the Empress can indicate that something is causing disruption or dissatisfaction in your home, a sense of pending loss, instability of resources, or overall lack of contentment. Reconnect with nature, focus on self-care if needed, and be compassionate in your relationships with others.

4 THE EMPEROR

The Emperor shows not only authority and law but also strength and power. This is the card of warmongers and leaders and represents taking decisive and deliberate action. When you see the Emperor card, it typically symbolizes a strong and assertive individual who offers guidance born from experience. Although that input may not always be wanted, it's usually worth paying attention to. This card is certainly one of direction and knowledge accumulated through a lifetime, as well as the empowerment needed when facing down conflict and challenges.

However, if the Emperor appears reversed in your reading, it can be a sign of someone who is losing control. Sometimes this means emotional rather than physical instability, but regardless, it often indicates that harm of some sort is coming. Consider whether asserting dominance is something important in your life or if you're willing to remove yourself from the spotlight and let others take center stage once in a while.

5   THE HIEROPHANT

When a Hierophant card comes up, look for an individual with a preference for ritual and ordered ceremony. In part, this could reflect a need for acceptance from others—possibly from society as a whole—or a desire for institutionalized approval. The Hierophant indicates the importance of conformity, guidelines, and structure. This card can be a reminder to study in a way that's focused and organized, particularly when it comes to spiritual beliefs, and learn from those who have experience rather than just winging it.

A reversed Hierophant, on the other hand, reveals people who are open minded and accepting of new ideas—people willing to think outside the box, even if it disregards cultural and societal norms to do so. This is the card of the non-conformist—the rebel, the hippie, the artist who colors outside the lines. Allow yourself to learn on your own when it serves you to do so, view the world through your own lens, and step away from traditions and values that no longer serve you.

6   THE LOVERS

The Lovers don't necessarily have to do with physical or romantic love, but this card can certainly be about relationships and the way we connect with the people in our lives who are the most important to us. Additionally, the Lovers is a card of choices and may indicate a situation in which we must decide something—or possibly even overcome temptation. The Lovers show us we have alternatives and that sometimes, decisions are hard to make. Keep all your alternatives in mind when the Lovers appear, and make sure whatever option you go with, you're true to your own needs, values, and overall well-being.

In reverse, the Lovers remind us that poor choices can lead to negative outcomes. Quarrels, and occasionally even infidelity spawned by temptation, can be revealed here. This card shows us it's time to stabilize our emotions and stop focusing on carnal desires. Think about whether your relationships are truly balanced in the way you need them to be, and if you—or the other person—are letting external influences or baggage get in the way of a harmonious and healthy connection.

7 THE CHARIOT

The Chariot card is another card of action. If it shows up in a Tarot spread, it indicates success and triumph. It's a card that says we are in control—sometimes even over things that we normally have no influence upon such as natural disasters, or other forces we can't change. If you're involved in business, this is a valuable card to see—it can mean that as long as you're willing to set boundaries, establish clear goals, and do the work, more responsibilities and the associated rewards could be on the way.

A reversed Chariot can symbolize a victory won by unethical means, such as cheating, lying, or manipulating others to get one's own way. It can also be a sign that instead of seeing opportunities, you're viewing everything as an obstacle. If your struggles seem overwhelming, take a step back and re-examine your own motivations. What do you hope to achieve and why? Once you become clear on these questions, you can move forward once more.

8 STRENGTH

Strength isn't only our physical prowess, it's also our spiritual determination and emotional fortitude. The Strength card reminds us our goals are in sight, and that with confidence and perseverance, we can overcome the challenges lying before us. Be patient and find it in yourself to keep going, and eventually your force of character will shine through. This is often a card of coping strategies, setting boundaries, and taking chances; it's also associated with loyalty and support toward those we love who may be struggling.

When the Strength card appears in the reversed position, it may be a sign of someone whose life is ruled less by emotion and spiritual balance and more by material needs and desires. Fear of the unknown can make you vulnerable and insecure, in addition to prompting you to act thoughtlessly. What steps will help you invest in self-care so you can rest, rejuvenate, and recover?

9 THE HERMIT

Standing alone with a lantern, the Hermit appears in a reading to let us know there are opportunities available to receive wisdom from the spirit world or the divine. This card reminds us that goals are attainable for those willing to put in the time and energy, but the journey isn't always going to be smooth or simple. It's a card of contemplation and inner reflection, prompting us to seek out answers where we once had only questions. The Hermit often represents opportunities for guidance, new journeys of self-discovery, and meditative self-evaluation.

A reversed Hermit card can reveal an individual unwilling to listen to wisdom from reliable sources. This person will disregard the advice of elders or more knowledgeable people, simply because they're not interested in learning from any experience other than their own. In particular, this can be a sign that you're self-isolating too much—take time to enjoy your solitude, but don't let yourself push away those who care about you. Hold space for yourself, but be mindful of letting others in.

10 THE WHEEL OF FORTUNE

The Wheel of Fortune reminds us we really do have the power to make changes in our own lives, even as the world is constantly shifting and fluid, and we don't have to be ruled by fate. Expect success thanks to some intelligent decisions, an improvement in luck, or significant creative evolution. Overall, it's a hopeful card that tells us we can make our own destiny—but also that we reap what we sow. Surround yourself with positive people and adopt an optimistic mindset, and you'll enjoy the rewards. Fill your life with negative thinking and unkindness, and that's what you'll attract.

Reversed, the Wheel indicates stagnation and setbacks. Unexpected conditions and changes will require you to be courageous and take some big steps, but remember the energy, effort, and time you put into any enterprise will be gratifying many times over. Own your mistakes and learn from them so they don't become habits.

11 JUSTICE

When Justice appears, know that fairness and balance will rule the day. Keep in mind, Justice isn't about what you want—it's about what is just, which means there's some accountability involved. Often associated with legal matters, this card represents the rule of law, and again, the outcome depends on your own actions. Sometimes this is a card of choices, so if you've got a big decision to make, be sure you make it in an informed manner so you know the full effect of your choice on both your own life and other people's lives. In some cases, the Justice card can show a desire for higher education—are you thinking about going back to school, studying a trade, or teaching others what you've learned?

In reverse, the Justice card highlights potential legal problems and complications. If you have a court case pending, this can be considered a likely unfavorable outcome. It also can be a reminder that when judging others, mercy and empathy can help us avoid being unnecessarily harsh. Learn to be compassionate toward yourself and those who are impacted by your decisions.

12 THE HANGED MAN

The Hanged Man, sometimes called The Hanged One, is seen as a highly significant card, and although many of its meanings are hidden, it can be deeply layered. This card reveals wisdom or prophetic knowledge we have not tapped or discovered, lying dormant beneath the surface. The Hanged Man tells us that sometimes, it's necessary to hit our internal pause button if we need to put things on hold. Learn to step back and evaluate these small breaks and see them as valuable and necessary rather than just plowing ahead. The universe wants you to stop and breathe.

Reversed, the Hanged Man reveals an individual with no interest in learning about spiritual growth and who refuses to accept the need for sacrifice to evolve and develop. Watch out that you don't become overly self-absorbed or too caught up in material matters. Remember there is a big difference between activity and productivity.

13 DEATH

This card, despite what you've likely seen in movies or on television, rarely signifies physical death. Instead, the Death card represents the endless cycle of life, death, and rebirth. It shows there is perpetual transformation, and we can reinvent ourselves and begin again at any time. This card reveals evolution and regeneration, creation following destruction. Welcome new opportunities, new ideas, and new beginnings.

In reverse, the Death card represents a tendency toward stagnation, never growing or moving forward, and remaining inert, without change. It can also show a resistance to changing or accepting new ideas. What baggage are you carrying around from the past, and how does it impact your current life and relationships? Learn to let go of the negative ideas, people, or things that hold you back and don't satisfy you. Clearing them out of your life will open room for new opportunities and growth.

14 TEMPERANCE

The Temperance card shows we can benefit when we alchemize imagination into activity, developing our will to bring about change. Temperance also reminds us to play nicely in the sandbox with others, and that teamwork—and even occasional compromise—can bring about achievement and success. It shows us balance through blending, unifying many elements to accomplish one shared goal.

When reversed, Temperance reveals some pretty poor circumstances—toxic relationships with other people, bad financial decisions, possibly even dishonesty or exploitation. See this as a warning: it's time to re-evaluate your situation and strive for a better balance. Stop overdoing yourself and stretching yourself too thin; instead, find a way to reprioritize so you can align your actions with your visions for the future.

15 THE DEVIL

If you see the Devil card in a Tarot spread, watch out for discontent and dangerous levels of obsession, emotional stagnation, or someone so tied to the material that they neglect the spiritual aspects of their lives. The Devil is a card associated with poor decision-making but may also appear as a representation of addiction or mental illness. However, the Devil can have positive attributes; this card can be a catalyst for breaking the chains that bind us.

In reverse, the Devil portrays a sunnier picture, showing the removal of the burden of material bondage in favor of spiritual understanding. Find ways to climb out of your darkness, illuminating your own path toward healing, courage, and growth.

16 THE TOWER

Tarot cards often show gradual evolutionary change, but the Tower reflects sudden, dramatic shifts—and much of them are because of forces completely external and out of your control. When the Tower emerges, it indicates big, often abrupt changes, conflict, and catastrophe. Prepare to rebuild because your world may be about to crash down; you'll be questioning everything you thought you knew and believed.

A reversed Tower shows that freedom of mind and spirit can be attained, but only at a great cost. There's a lot of upheaval involved, which isn't uncommon in times of crisis. This may indicate someone hoping to break free of an abusive relationship or leave a disastrous job situation, but it's also a nudge to stop clinging to things that are unhealthy and unsatisfying. Quit fighting change, embrace it, and recognize that a new you will emerge from the ashes.

17 THE STAR

The Star is a card of meditation. It serves to show us that if we listen more than we speak, the truth will ultimately be revealed. This is the card of someone who is seeking and attaining inspiration, illumination, and insight. The Star sees hopeful possibilities instead of problems, opportunities rather than insurmountable obstacles. It's a card of giving, sharing, and unselfish compassion for others.

When in reverse, the Star reveals pessimism, doubt, and cynicism. It represents someone who lacks the perception to grow spiritually or emotionally and always sees the glass as half empty. It can indicate discontent with the things that used to bring satisfaction; figure out how to nourish your spirit and soul so you can find joy once more.

18 THE MOON

If you see the Moon card in a Tarot spread, watch for the development of dormant psychic abilities. The Moon can represent hidden messages and deception, as well as imagination and intuition. Things are not always as they seem on the surface, so when this card appears, trust your instinct, especially when it relates to trauma and fear from your past.

When the Moon appears in reverse, it could be a sign that your intuition and psychic abilities have been blocked or repressed in the past, but you've been dealing with the blockages and repression and are trying to heal. While things may not make sense right now, take time to listen to your own instinct rather than let others exert undue influence upon you. Soon, you'll find the right path to take and be more open to the messages the universe is sending.

19 THE SUN

The Sun is nearly always a sign of good things to come; it's the card of happy families, healthy relationships, and mental and physical well-being. For students and scholars, it can reflect the freedom—and relief—that comes with completing studies and learning. The Sun reminds us there can be great joy found in the simplest of things. If this card appears in your reading, the future is bright indeed!

In reverse, the Sun card may symbolize a cloudy future. It can point to someone who is wandering about with no clear goals in sight, or whose marriage or job could be facing potential risk. It's only a temporary setback, though; eventually, you'll get refocused and find your groove again.

20 Judgment

The Judgment card indicates someone who has worked to intentionally cultivate a rewarding life full of joy and contentment and weathered the bumpy roads on their journey to advancement. It reveals awakening and renewal—not just spiritually, but also emotionally and physically. This card shows we've experienced a change in personal perception and gained a new ability to blend with our world. Everything is beginning to come together, falling into place in a way that will lead you to your true self. Judgment can also symbolize favorable legal outcomes.

Reversed, the Judgment card shows our fears and weaknesses. In particular, it can reveal someone whose avoidance of commitment can lead to a failure in finding happiness. It may even indicate the end of a marriage or other relationship, as well as a loss of material possessions. Learn to set aside your self-doubt and all the other things holding you back so you can embrace transformational, positive change.

21 The World

This is the final card in the Major Arcana, and as you may imagine, it symbolizes completion, freedom and liberation, and triumph in all undertakings. It lets us know we're about to achieve our goals, and all of our efforts will finally pay off as everything falls into place. But the adventure doesn't end here—take some time to reflect on your successes, celebrate your accomplishments, and think about what you've learned along the way.

Reversed, the World shows success has yet to be attained, often because of an unwillingness to move on and let go of the past. This can indicate someone overly attached to their home or job, refusing to take chances with new opportunities. Think about the many steps you need to take to accomplish your dreams, and then tackle them in small increments, one at a time, until the process becomes more manageable.

7
The Suit of Cups

In Tarot, Cup cards are related to the element of water. Like water, this suit is fluid, connected to our emotions, creativity, and interpersonal relationships, as well as healing, cleansing, and purification. Think of the Cup cards as those that represent aspects of our lives driven by feelings over logic, making decisions and taking actions based upon emotion rather than reason. If you lay out cards in a spread and see many Cups, it could mean you're seeking answers to questions about interpersonal relationships, emotional matters, or creative endeavors.

One/Ace of Cups

Aces are always seen as a sign of a new beginning in Tarot, and the Ace of Cups can show us the possibilities of new friendships or other meaningful, loving personal relationships. This card is also associated with creativity, spiritual insight, and good fortune. It tells us great blessings—even miracles—are beginning to take place. It reminds us that when we invest in our connections with others, we can feel an abundance of riches.

When the Ace of Cups appears in reverse, all of those happy insight gets twisted, revealing disenchantment or sadness, although not necessarily our own. Sometimes, it tells us we need to be cautious of other people's feelings. Have you said something hurtful—or failed to express kindness and love—to someone you care about?

Two of Cups

The Two of Cups represents the development of an existing relationship—soul mates, close friends, etc. It could even be tied to a relationship you don't yet know is significant; is there someone in your life you'd like to know better? Focus on the connections you already have, and work on strengthening and enhancing them, establishing bonds through harmony.

When the Two of Cups is reversed, it reveals a disagreement has caused a rift, so it's time to mend fences! Usually, it's a simple misunderstanding that has led to division between people. Is there an individual you're squabbling with over something insignificant? Be the bigger person and try extending a hand in peace so you can have a more fulfilling relationship.

Three of Cups

The Three of Cups is a celebratory card. It shows merriment, rejoicing, and happy events shared with those you love the most. Spend time with the people who lift you up and support you rather than push you down, and embrace each other's victories and triumphs. Work together collaboratively for common goals within your community.

If the Three of Cups appears reversed, it could be a sign that discord and disharmony are at play here—not through any maliciousness, but usually because of personality conflicts. Sometimes it means you need a break from other people, so invest in your solitude for a while until you're ready to face the world. When you do, leave your baggage at home, and don't let bad feelings ruin the day for yourself or anyone else.

Four of Cups

Is it time to put things on hold for a little while? The Four of Cups is associated with a period of inactivity and dormancy. If you're feeling a lack of motivation, it may be time for some soul searching. In addition, this card can indicate a relationship with strings attached, so you'll need to establish guidelines and boundaries before things progress any further. Will you be expected to give more than you're receiving? Are you someone who prefers the other person to do the emotional heavy lifting?

Reversed, this card can mean it's time to wrap up your period of reflection or withdrawal and finally move forward. Think about whether you need to end a relationship neither party finds beneficial or step away from projects that don't bring you joy. Sometimes things just run their course, and there's no need to drag it out. Set new goals for yourself.

FIVE OF CUPS

When the Five of Cups appears, some sort of turmoil is brewing. Everything is a disappointment, even things that once made you happy. This card can also reveal indecision, regret, or disillusionment; specifically, it may represent someone who is torn between two choices, which means sacrifices need to be made.

In reverse, the Five of Cups still indicates a sacrifice will be made, but not as emotional in nature. Often, this means you're giving up something–or someone–you weren't really that attached to in the first place. Accept that it's time to move on, and set your expectations high.

SIX OF CUPS

When the Six of Cups card appears, it indicates incidents from the past are significantly impacting the present and even the future in a positive way. These events may be as far back as your childhood, or at the very least, several years ago, and the card may hint at a reuniting with an old friend, renewing long-forgotten interests, or forging ahead with dreams you'd once set aside.

When the Six of Cups appears in reverse, there's still influence from the past, but it's bogging you down. It can also reveal ways in which someone no longer in your life still maintains an emotional hold over you. Are you refusing to let go of your baggage and carrying around outdated emotions? It's time to learn from your mistakes.

Seven of Cups

The Seven of Cups is a card of opportunities and abundance, but be sure you make decisions based on the overall picture rather than short-term, immediate rewards. Planning and forethought will win the day over impulsive choices. Don't be distracted by new, shiny things if they won't serve you or bring you joy in the long run.

In reverse, the Seven of Cups reveals you may need to reprioritize. If you have too many difficult decisions to make, rely on your intuition and trust your gut. Stay focused and motivated, and with some resolve and determination, you'll be able to turn things around and push forward.

Eight of Cups

The Eight of Cups often represents someone who's aimlessly wandering and seeking but never manages to settle in one place or with one person for long. If something is lacking in your life, it's time to start looking for it, but first, you need to deal with your issues and problems. Figure out what's been holding you back and preventing you from finding what you need.

Reversed, the Eight of Cups reminds us to stop basing our choices on others' needs and wants. Prioritize your own emotions, which will allow you to welcome new joys and move toward success. Be cautious, though. A reversed Eight of Cups could represent someone focusing so much on material abundance they lose sight of spiritual and emotional blessings.

Nine of Cups

The Nine of Cups is one Tarot readers often refer to as a "wish card." As in, if this card comes up, you may just get your wish, and things are going great—you're right where you need to be! It's time to enjoy the experience of a life filled with satisfaction and blessings. Be sure to appreciate your blessings; gratitude is a crucial part of abundance and can lead to even more positive results.

A reversed Nine of Cups can serve as a cautionary card. Avoid getting complacent; you may be taking your relationships and family for granted, and that mindset can cause damage later. Don't overindulge and get carried away just because something seems great on the surface.

Ten of Cups

The Ten of Cups is generally recognized as a card of "happily ever after." It symbolizes the delight that comes when long-term relationships flourish and grow; it represents peace and contentment, happiness, dreams coming true, and sustainable joy. Family and relationship bonds are strong and secure and will withstand the tests of time.

In reverse, the Ten of Cups can reveal domestic stress on the way, and it could foreshadow a disruption in your home life. Things will work out eventually, but it will take some patience and occasional compromise. It can also indicate a betrayal from an unexpected source—are you placing your trust in someone who doesn't deserve it?

Page of Cups

Pages in Tarot are considered messengers, and the Page of Cups usually means someone is trying to get your attention—perhaps in matters of love or other relationships. It could represent an individual who is thoughtful and passionate or someone young at heart. The Page of Cups can also mean a message regarding a happy family-related event or an exciting creative endeavor.

The reversed Page of Cups is the upright Page of Cups' immature twin sibling. Someone may want you to notice them, but their methods may not always reflect the best choices. It can indicate stagnation, deception, obstacles, or upcoming unpleasant news. You might feel rudderless, like you're just drifting; what can you do to find a new direction?

Knight of Cups

The Knight of Cups is honorable but not warlike; it can symbolize someone who knows how to stand their ground but will not deliberately pick a fight. The Knight of Cups can also represent a blooming passion, such as artistic creativity or a new lover. It's a card of action that reminds us to follow through if we want to bring our dreams to fruition.

In reverse, the Knight of Cups is a warning about people who want attention just to serve their own needs. Sometimes people maneuver their way into our world without our best interests at heart, and the Knight of Cups advises caution. Is there an individual who has suddenly inserted themselves into your life? Stay connected to the reality of your situation rather than what you wish it to be.

Queen of Cups

The Queen of Cups is captivating, sensual, understanding, and naturally compelling. It's a card of vision, kindness, sturdiness, reliability, and strength. When this card appears, it may mean people see you as nurturing and genuine. Does everybody want to tell you their problems because you're a great listener? This card often represents a person who is an excellent provider of support and solutions.

Reversed, the Queen of Cups indicates an individual plagued by insecurity and self-doubt who uses others' vulnerabilities to achieve personal gain. There's a sense of selfishness, as well as unreliability and volatility, masked by intelligence. Are your emotions causing you to lose control?

King of Cups

The King of Cups shows us a social and outgoing individual, a creative type who loves to entertain others. This is a card of security, stability, and grounded home life that can also indicate a person's giving spirit, generous heart, and willingness to take responsibility for one's actions. The King of Cups is often the card of artists, musicians, and spiritual seekers and represents the ideal blend of emotion and reason.

Reversed, a King of Cups shows us deep insecurities, toxic relationships, and even narcissism. There can be ruthlessness, and even abusive traits, beneath the façade of an even, rational temper. Find your inner strength to prevent others from taking advantage of you physically, financially, or emotionally.

8
The Suit of Swords

The suit of Swords is related to the element of air in the Tarot; it's ever changing and shifting, constantly in motion, and tied to power, change, and conflict. The Swords represent aspects of our lives driven by action, ambition, and courage. If you find yourself looking at a large number of Swords in your Tarot layout, it may mean you're seeking answers to questions about internal or external struggles, upcoming challenges, intellectual matters, and solid and firm decision-making.

Ace/One of Swords

When the Ace of Swords appears, it usually means victory is imminent. Your success didn't happen on its own, it's something you earned through hard work and dedication. Now you'll see the efforts pay off as struggles shift to triumph. This card encourages us to try new things—after all, if you've been successful recently, why not continue to ride the wave? Move forward with the mindset that failure is not an option.

If the Ace of Swords appears in reverse, you may be pushing yourself too hard and overdoing yourself in your quest for success. It's time to sit back and chill out; just let things simmer for a while. If your efforts involve other people, someone is going to get hurt if you keep pressing. This card can also be a sign that others may be keeping you from your goals. Reevaluate the situation at hand and figure out if the problem is really with other people or simply with yourperception.

Two of Swords

The Two of Swords can represent someone who has put up an emotional wall as a defense mechanism. Is it preventing you from enjoying all the good things that might be coming your way? Think about whether your own barriers are stopping you from advancing. If you've been procrastinating or refusing to see the big picture, you need to decide something, or nothing will ever change.

When reversed, the Two of Swords often reveals that overprotectiveness; either of yourself or others is the source of a rift. Are you between a rock and a hard place because you're beingsmothering? Learn to give people the benefit of the doubt once in a while; you can protect those you love without stifling them.

Three of Swords

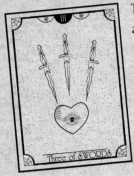

The Three of Swords is generally a card of discontent, hurt, and disappointment, often to do with failing or struggling relationships. Are you feeling conflicted about whether there should be someone else in the picture? Get ready for upheaval in your world, but remember that sorrow can help us grow. Plan to evaluate your relationships and make decisions to improve them when you see this card.

If your Three of Swords appears reversed, it means there might be hope for salvaging things after all. Choose your words wisely, and remember listening is as important as speaking; you might well be able to resolve those petty squabbles for the good. Remember that while you don't have control over other people's words or deeds, you do have power over how you respond to them.

Four of Swords

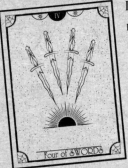

If the Four of Swords appears in your Tarot reading, it's time to recuperate before you collapse. How can you enjoy the fruits of your labor if you're overwhelmed? Emotional and physical exhaustion can affect people in so many ways. Give yourself a break and the gift of time to recharge and rejuvenate; it will boost your confidence and give you a fresh perspective.

In reverse, the Four of Swords hints you are past the phase of collapse being imminent; you're worn out, burned out, and just plain beat. A crash is underway, and if you don't find some balance, you'll just continue to be frustrated. Find ways to calm your inner critic so you can look toward the future instead of dwell on the past.

Five of Swords

The Five of Swords is typically seen as a card of conflict and often shows up to let us know about a falling out. It's time to mend fences and own it when you've wronged another person or hurt their feelings. Learn to pick your battles because sometimes winning has a cost. This card can also indicate a betrayal is imminent; do you trust everyone who's around you?

In reverse, a Five of Swords can reveal someone who won't let go of an argument, even when it's time to move on. The fight is over, the point has been made, and everyone knows everyone else's opinion. Now it's time to stop beating the dead horse; don't gloat over a victory or carry a grudge about a defeat.

Six of Swords

The Six of Swords is a transitional card, an indicator that life is on the upswing. You've survived the battle, and things are going to get better. Not only is your situation improving, but you're also developing as a person, which better equips you to form coping strategies for the future. It can be hard to shed the trauma and damage of the past, but once you're able to do so, your personal growth will flourish.

When the Six of Swords appears in reverse, life may be improving, but perhaps not as fast as you'd like. What can you do differently to speed things along? Try not to be overly resistant to change. Is there someone you need to talk to, or an action that must take place before things normalize? Start forward, resolve your unfinished business, and get things done.

Seven of Swords

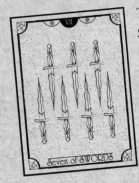

The Seven of Swords typically indicates deception and betrayal. Someone is deliberately being untruthful with you. Do you trust everyone in your circle? Is someone keeping secrets from you? Whether this deception is in your personal life or your professional one, it's crucial to be strategic in how you proceed. Just because others are untrustworthy doesn't mean you should respond in kind. Instead, be the better person and take the high road.

The Seven of Swords reversed indicates that even if you're feeling left out or disappointed, it's not because other people are malicious. No one was trying to be sneaky or deliberately exclude you; they simply didn't think. There's no ill intent going on here. If you've got your own secrets you're keeping from others, it's time to come clean.

Eight of Swords

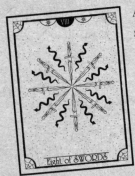

Are you having trouble achieving your goals? The Eight of Swords shows us our own fear of failure can hold us back. New things can be scary—after all, the idea of not succeeding is terrifying for some of us—but if you never take the steps, you'll never move forward. Accept the risk, stop overthinking things, and make things happen for yourself. Don't blame other people for your lack of progress; it's up to you to do the work.

A reversed Eight of Swords indicates you'll be moving forward if you can just learn to deal with your own worries and doubts. Poor self-esteem and negative perceptions of your own worth can hold you back. As you learn to be less frustrated with the shortcomings of other people, you'll also discover ways to celebrate your successes more and accept that you deserve to be happy.

Nine of Swords

The Nine of Swords is often associated with poor mental health and overwhelming sadness and grief. If you don't have anyone to talk to about what's causing that inner pain, you need to find someone right now. A shared burden is a little bit easier to carry, and it helps to have support. Talk to a trusted friend or family member so you don't have to deal with things alone.

In reverse, the Nine of Swords is very similar to the upright interpretation in that it indicates a need to reach out for a hand up when you're down in the pit. However, a reversed Nine of Swords is stronger, and it means you may need a professional level of intervention. Don't be afraid to ask for assistance getting back on track; if you're thinking about harming yourself or others, make the call for help right away.

Ten of Swords

The Ten of Swords can be a portent of grief. Something is coming to an end, whether it's the finality of a broken relationship, the death of a loved one, or the loss of something else deeply important to you. Often, it's a card of heartache and sadness, in part because of the loss itself and in part because of the realization that things are over. It can also serve as a reminder that even after the darkest part of the night, the sun eventually rises; when things are terrible, they'll gradually improve, but it will likely hurt much along the way.

Feeling optimistic even when times are bad? When you see a Ten of Swords in reverse, it shows us light at the end of the tunnel. Look around and figure out how you can face the situation head on, releasing yourself from the heartache and finding a renewed sense of purpose and hope.

PAGE OF SWORDS

The Page of Swords serves as a high-energy messenger, telling us to figure out what matters most in our lives. Where are your passion and excitement, and how can you channel it into a new and gratifying project? Once you decide where your talent lies, share your enthusiasm and excitement with others.

The reversed Page of Swords is a messenger card, too, but this time it brings less pleasant tidings. It can indicate hasty decisions, a lack of commitment, or even an imposter who claims to know more than they really do. Is there someone in your life making immature, erratic, or uninformed decisions? If so, avoid them—when they crash and burn, they're going to bring you down with them.

KNIGHT OF SWORDS

The Knight of Swords is associated with chivalry and symbolizes loyalty, determination, and strong convictions. It's a card of motivation and assertive action rather than reaction but also serves as a reminder that spontaneous decisions need to be balanced with forethought and planning. This card can also indicate we need to pay attention to the truth, even when we don't like what we're seeing.

A reversed Knight of Swords warns us that when we get overly wrapped up in things, it can sometimes lead to frustration. You're so excited about so much, you can't focus enough to complete a task. Watch out for others' hurt feelings. Is your passion for something new making people around you feel abandoned?

Queen of Swords

The Queen of Swords signifies balanced opinions and just decisions and often represents someone well-respected but not necessarily approachable. Are you shutting people out, presenting the image that you think too highly of yourself? Others may like and admire you but also find you intimidating because of your no-nonsense, straight-to-the-point attitude.

If you see this card in reverse, the Queen of Swords can represent judgmental and narrow-minded behavior, perhaps even a bit of malice. This could be someone who refuses to listen to new ideas because of their own inflexibility—in other words, someone who sticks to tradition for tradition's sake. Learn to be more objective toward the situation at hand.

King of Swords

The King of Swords is a card of authority and intellect; it also symbolizes truth, fairness, and honor. Often, the King represents someone whose knowledge and wisdom you can learn from—look for guidance based on facts and data, not feelings or emotions. This card can represent the subject matter experts; the professional consultants who lack personal involvement in your situation often are the best to give objective advice.

The King of Swords in reverse can show a lack of flexibility and occasional misuse of power. A reversed King of Swords could reflect a person who comes across as harsh or judgmental just because of their own inability to be tolerant of new people or concepts. Are you giving others a fair chance at communicating with you, or are you automatically rejecting their ideas just because they aren't your own?

9

THE SUIT OF WANDS

Associated with the element of fire, the cards within the suit of
Wands are passionate and full of raw energy. It's the suit of both
creation and destruction and is associated with human will, our
desires and ambitions, and our energy and ego. Wands represent
aspects of our lives motivated by achievement and determination
and driven by thoughts and ideas. If you encounter a large
number of Wands in your Tarot layout, it could mean the
universe is trying to tell you about your energy, passion,
motivation, communication, and life goals.

Ace/One of Wands

When the Ace of Wands appears, it's usually a sign of new beginnings and new energies. Is your gut telling you it's time to take on a new challenge or opportunity? Follow your instinct because this is a card of brand-new adventures. But every journey begins with a single step. Map out your path and see where the road will take you.

When the Ace of Wands appears reversed, it could be a sign to delay your big plans—but only temporarily. If this is the case, don't panic; let things sit for a little while as you figure out what really drives you, and you're far more likely to have success.

Two of Wands

When the Two of Wands appears, it can indicate a growth in new partnerships and relationships, and these are likely to benefit everyone involved. This is often related to your career or business instead of romantic, social, or familial relationships. Are you thinking about seeking out a promotion or furthering your education? It's time to really get serious about exploring your options for the future.

When the Two of Wands is reversed, it can show us we've been sitting around waiting for far too long. Stop wishing for opportunities to come your way, and go out and look for them. Proactive rather than reactive movement will be to your benefit. Be more assertive without being aggressive; otherwise, all your big ideas will never be anything more than unfulfilled wishes. Don't be afraid to challenge the unknown.

THREE OF WANDS

The Three of Wands is a card of success. Think about all you've put your hard work, time, and energy into. The Three of Wands says your ship is about to come in because effort and diligence reap their own rewards. Stay on target, but step outside your normal sphere of comfort if necessary. It's okay to be proud of your accomplishments, and if some of your success is due to others' labors, be sure they share in the accolades. Give credit for collaborative partnerships.

When your Three of Wands shows up reversed, it's an indication that you're a bit stagnant because you're prioritizing the security of the familiar over the risk of change. Get motivated, get focused, and get moving, and you'll see transformation as you set goals and become more proactive. Be cautious, though; not everyone who offers to help you has your best interest in mind.

FOUR OF WANDS

When a Four of Wands appears in the Tarot, it's time to celebrate! You're entitled to feel joy and happiness. You deserve it because you've earned it, and good times are here. Don't diminish the things you've accomplished or are about to achieve. If you've been burning the midnight oil, allow yourself to take a breather and get some rest; it will help you find balance and security in the long run.

A reversed Four of Wands can represent lethargy and overall indifference; if you're really feeling listless, get some friends involved. This card may reveal uncertainty about what the future holds. If you're about to face big life changes—switching jobs, ending or starting a relationship, buying a home—realize a sense of fear and anxiety is a normal response.

Five of Wands

When the Five of Wands appears, it means you need to take steps to end the discord and disagreements. Clear the air, but also be honest about what you're feeling. The Five of Wands reminds us we have to be authentic if we want the conflict to cease, both with others and with ourselves. Remember, competition can sometimes be healthy as long as it's collaborative; welcome the opinions and insights others can bring to the table.

In reverse, the Five of Wands hints at someone who avoids conflict. Got an argument that's dragging on for ages? That's because you keep changing your opinion or refuse to stand firm and commit to what you believe. Compromise and a willingness to learn and grow is fine but refusing to take any side at all might alienate and anger people around you.

Six of Wands

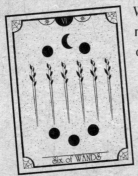

When the Six of Wands shows up, success is at hand—and there's more than internal satisfaction. There's also public recognition of your accomplishments. Others will acknowledge your contributions and help celebrate your hard work, so take the credit when it's due and don't downplay your efforts. There will still be challenges on the road ahead, but you're past the tough part, and you've got a support team to help out if you need it.

If the Six of Wands appears reversed, you may still experience a win, but it could be a bittersweet one. In this case, success could even have its disadvantages. Did you ride someone else's coattails or receive praise you didn't truly earn? Are you worried pride in your accomplishments might be viewed by others as bragging and boasting?

Seven of Wands

The Seven of Wands tells us the competition is about to get tough, and you're going to need to brace yourself. Muster up your inner strength if you want to see a victory because you're up against people with plenty of fortitude of their own. Have a worst-case-scenario plan in place in the event things don't go your way. To be an effective leader, play by the rules, but give it your all. Watch out for the competition because not everyone plays fair.

The reversed Seven of Wands reminds us that self-doubt can often sabotage our efforts. It serves as a warning that our sense of inadequacy can cause failure in both professional and personal endeavors. Work on building your own confidence before you feel threatened, or you may end up being your own worst enemy.

Eight of Wands

Be glad when the Eight of Wands presents itself: it's a card of revitalization and passion! Everything is about to kick back into high gear; the Eight of Wands is a card of success all the way around, whether it has to do with your career, creative goals, or even your sex life. This card represents advancement, excitement, and rapid movement.

When the Eight of Wands is reversed, things are coming to a screeching halt. Stagnation and indecision—possibly even jealousy—are going to hold you back, and nothing will move ahead. If you truly want to bring about change, you'd better re-evaluate the situation and your response to it. Take a holistic approach, focusing on the needs of your mind, body, and spirit, and things will begin to shift in your favor.

Nine of Wands

If you've got a Nine of Wands in your spread, you may be handling adversity well, but you're probably viewing things through a skeptical lens. Stop letting doubt overshadow your successes. Questioning things is part of life, but don't let this prevent you from moving forward. Be resilient and stay on your journey, even when others try to lead you down the wrong path.

In reverse, the Nine of Wands tells us those suspicions we've had all along may actually be rooted in the truth. Got doubts about something or someone? You're probably right. Now that you know what's really going on, plan your response thoughtfully and strategically. This card can also indicate you're feeling overwhelmed; don't start any more projects until you finish some of the ones in progress.

Ten of Wands

A Ten of Wands often shows up as a word of caution: it's a warning not to bite off more than you can chew. You may find yourself physically and mentally exhausted if you take on additional responsibilities and burdens, especially other people's. Learn to delegate, or you're never going to get your head above water.

In reverse, the Ten of Wands reminds us to let the past be the past—and that includes all the baggage you were dragging along. Once things are over, give yourself (and others) a break if necessary. It may also be a sign there will be some loss in the future; what things or people are on their way out of your life?

Page of Wands

Like the other Pages, the Page of Wands is a messenger card and usually means good news is on the way—opportunities abound! This card also means the truth will soon reveal itself. If you've been worried about deception, now is when you'll find out the real deal. You might be surprised—or even relieved—by what you learn.

The reversed Page of Wands still tells us news is on the way, but this time it indicates the news is from an unexpected source. Be sure to validate the information you receive and consider the person who gave it to you—do they have something to gain by telling you?

Knight of Wands

Like all Knights in the Tarot, the Knight of Wands is chivalrous, but this card indicates someone who is soul searching and needs to discover the truth on their own without others' machinations. It's a card of courage and risks to be taken, and of drawing unbiased conclusions. Make sure you have all the information you need before proceeding.

In reverse, the Knight of Wands cautions us against being too extreme in our passions; it can lead to frustration and temperamental behavior. This card advises us to own our mistakes and apologize to those we have wronged. Learn to be less impulsive and more thoughtful.

Queen of Wands

The Queen of Wands is a card of inspiration and energy and may symbolize someone who makes everyone feel welcomed, liked, and valued. This is an individual who never makes themself feel superior by insulting or belittling others. This card represents kindness, generosity, and genuine compassion for the rest of the world.

When in reverse, the Queen of Wands is still outgoing and social, but far more manipulative. This could be a person whose interactions with others are based on what benefit they can attain; if they can get nothing from you, they won't bother interacting. Beware of people who are friendly on the surface, yet unscrupulous underneath.

King of Wands

The King of Wands may represent a person with a powerful and dominant personality but who still manages to remain friendly and nonjudgmental. This person is open and social, but more importantly, they're truly genuine in their interactions with others. Often a card of leaders, it can reflect someone who's a visionary and is excellent at inspiring others to work together for a shared goal.

The King of Wands in reverse shows someone who lacks basic people skills. They may be excellent at their job but cannot read social and nonverbal cues from others. This type of individual can be highly successful as long as their advancement is based on merit rather than interaction with teammates or collaborators. Watch to make sure you're not being too aggressive in the way you network; lead by example, not by barking orders.

10

The Suit of Pentacles/Coins

The cards of the suit of Pentacles—sometimes portrayed as Coins—are connected with the element of earth and all of the stability, security, and abundance that comes along with it. The cards reflect our need for balance between our spiritual development and material possessions and are associated with the ego and our self-esteem; Pentacles are often self-image driven. This suit is all about practicality, generosity, and building our lives up to where we desire to be. When a layout features many Pentacles, it may mean you seek solutions to situations related to your financial well-being, material objects, and security.

Ace/One of Pentacles

When the Ace of Pentacles appears, there's a sense of prosperity on the horizon, but it's not going to be just handed to you. You'll have to work to earn it—it's up to you to reach for the opportunity when it presents itself. This can signify the beginning of new wealth, whether it's in the form of a job or an investment opportunity. Remember that money you've worked hard for spends just as well as money that comes from an unexpected source. Additionally, there are many different interpretations of what "abundance" means; it may not be financial, but there's still a chance for overall fulfillment.

When the Ace of Pentacles is reversed, it can reflect a false start, especially related to your career or financial situation. Do your homework and recognize that not all financial opportunities are to your benefit in the long run. Watch out for people whose investment ideas are fraudulent, and be sure to plan ahead for potential financial setbacks.

Two of Pentacles

Like many Twos in the Tarot, the Two of Pentacles can be a card of choices. It often indicates someone who is juggling many different aspects of their lives—and doing a good job at it! But make sure you don't overdo it and stretch yourself too thin. Slow things down a little bit so you can prioritize your responsibilities. Watch out that you don't start "robbing Peter to pay Paul" when it comes to your money obligations.

When reversed, this card warns you could find yourself in a situation that's out of your control, which can lead to an inability to maintain balance. Make sure you don't waste time trying to present others with a false image of a perfect life if you're barely keeping it together. Get yourself organized and set clear boundaries and priorities for your finances and obligations.

Three of Pentacles

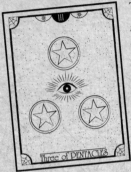

The Three of Pentacles is a sign to collaborate with others to achieve big results. This card shows us that as we implement plans, we can accomplish what we set out to if we all work together as a team. It's a card of encouragement, reflecting the material increase that will appear if we plan ahead and delegate tasks based upon each participant's skills and knowledge.

When your Three of Pentacles shows up reversed, you may be encountering difficulty finishing what you started because there's disharmony or selfishness in your team. Everyone is so preoccupied with their own needs that they're ignoring the good of the whole. Find a way to make sure everyone's contributions are being valued, and encourage respect and fairness among the team.

Four of Pentacles

If the Four of Pentacles appears, there's material gain and bounty present but also a bit of miserliness and greed. Are you so focused on accumulating and hoarding abundance that you've alienated people that matter to you? Start thinking about how you can share wealth with others; learn the art of generosity and determine what sort of legacy you wish to leave behind.

The reversed Four of Pentacles can indicate a loss of financial status. Is your spending so out of control that you can't pay your bills? Buying things doesn't always bring happiness. In fact, it can create a whole new set of problems as you find yourself running short of resources. In some cases, this card indicates someone who has realized material things aren't important to them anymore; a subsequent reduction in possessions is part of redefining their relationship with money.

Five of Pentacles

When the Five of Pentacles appears, watch out for devastating financial loss; a loss of a job or even a home creates a lack of security for the future. In this case, we tend to focus on a scarcity mindset, and we concentrate so much on what we don't have that we can't think about the things we need or want. This is a card of loneliness brought on by destitution, a spiritual dark night of the soul.

A reversed Five of Pentacles shows us the hard times are coming to an end. There may be a charity to help out or friends lending a helping hand or even a new job allowing you to get back on your feet. It's a card of hopefulness, showing us life truly is worth living and that our happiness isn't defined by the size of our bank accounts. In many cases, it can lead to a renewed interest in our spiritual growth and development.

Six of Pentacles

The Six of Pentacles is a reminder that giving to others feels good. Giving doesn't have to be financial because our time and energy can have as much value as our money. A mindset of charitable giving is spiritually fulfilling, especially when you know every contribution you give can make a difference in someone else's life. This is also a card of gratitude; in addition to giving generously, learn to receive with thankfulness, and show appreciation for those who lifted you up when you were down.

When the Six of Pentacles appears in reverse, it tells us to give to ourselves if we need it, especially if we've been freely giving to others. Watch out for gifts that are given to you with conditions; these aren't truly gifts, and people could be taking advantage of your kindness. Protect your assets by avoiding the addition of new debts or financial obligations.

Seven of Pentacles

When you see a Seven of Pentacles, it shows us that it's time to reap what we have sown. It's a card of planning for the future so we can enjoy the long-term benefits—but remember, sometimes life is a marathon, not a sprint. Step back and pause for a moment, look at the big picture, and realize that success could soon be on the horizon if we stay on task. It's okay to take a break now and then if you need it.

The Seven of Pentacles in reverse can reflect impatience; sure, you've been working hard, but when will it ever pay off? Ask yourself whether you're channeling your efforts into the right places—if there's no return on investment, maybe you need to walk away. Is your work making you anxious and angry? It's okay to admit when you discover there's no success forthcoming.

Eight of Pentacles

The Eight of Pentacles is often a card of growth and knowledge. While there may be a profitable enterprise coming in the future, you'll need to put all your energy into mastering the skills you need to bring your goal to fruition. If you've recently changed jobs, gone back to school, or experienced a shift in financial circumstances, it's time to concentrate hard and become a master of your field.

A reversed Eight of Pentacles indicates someone so focused on improvement and perfection that the goals become unrealistic and unattainable. Quit worrying about the minuscule details that don't matter, and get back to looking toward the bigger picture. False vanity and impractical expectations will lead to a failure in realizing your ambitions as well as preventing you from adapting and growing where you need to.

Nine of Pentacles

The Nine of Pentacles represents accomplishment. It shows us we've attained the wisdom we need to enjoy our successes, as well as the material comforts to provide us with a secure, happy life. By establishing a stable foundation for our material well-being, we can sit back, breathe, and enjoy ourselves! The Nine of Pentacles often reveals someone who has overcome challenges, rebuilt after a disaster, and is perfectly content to exist in solitude. This card reminds us of the difference between being happily alone versus unhappily lonely.

A reversed Nine of Pentacles often indicates that while we may be working hard, it may not be to our own benefit. Are there other people taking advantage of you or stealing all the credit for your efforts? You deserve to enjoy the fruits of your labor, so watch out for people who would manipulate you for their own gain. This card can also indicate someone living beyond their means in hopes of achieving social status. Stop spending money you don't have just to impress the neighbors or gain influence.

Ten of Pentacles

In many traditions of Tarot, the Ten of Pentacles celebrates our achievements, whether they're related to work, investments, or other material matters. Hard work has created a sense of permanence and a maintainable future. This is a card of family—not just regarding the relationships we have created and are maintaining, but also regarding the ability we have to provide for those we love. The Ten of Pentacles is associated with long-term success and happy, stable homes.

Reversed, the Ten of Pentacles warns us of misfortune, often related to family and finance. When we surround ourselves with material stuff—especially if we do it to impress others—we may end up dissatisfied with what we have. Don't get involved in high-risk projects if it means you could endanger your family's security.

Page of Pentacles

The Page of Pentacles—like all Pages, a messenger—tells us to be aware of money's value, careers, and new ideas that can help us manifest additional abundance. It's a card revealing endless possibilities and potential, all of which can materialize if we're willing to take the necessary actions. The Page of Pentacles prompts us toward learning and education; by expanding our knowledge and wisdom, we can make our dreams come true.

The reversed Page of Pentacles points to someone who is far too invested in life's material aspects. While there may be new projects or ideas on the horizon, you won't be able to launch them forward because you've lost track of inspiration and intention, too focused on the material instead.

Knight of Pentacles

The Knight of Pentacles represents hard work and perseverance, effort in the face of repetitive and tedious labor, and responsibility. This is the card of the detail-oriented, the organized, and the methodical planners. While change might be coming soon, you'll get the best results if you stick to familiar tasks, establish a predictable routine, and keep your head down until it's time to celebrate success.

In reverse, the Knight of Pentacles is still scheduled and routine, but to the point that progress never happens. Stagnation doesn't move you forward, so try new ideas to see if you get better results. This card also reminds us not to have unrealistic expectations of others if we want their help in achieving our goals; when things are finished, people will remember how you treat them and could be less supportive in the future if they were treated poorly.

Queen of Pentacles

The Queen of Pentacles signifies a blend between the stability of domestic life and the security of hard work and effort. It can represent someone who can balance the practical needs of labor with the emotional ones of the family. An archetype often associated with working parents, it's a card of generosity and abundance but also of the wise and productive use of talents and skills.

When in reverse, the Queen of Pentacles can reveal a neglect of duties—either at work, at home, or both. Are you putting too much of your attention in one area to the detriment of the other, or depending on other people to fill in the gaps you've created? Has an awareness of this lack of balance caused you to experience a sense of failure, or that you're not good enough as a parent, partner, employee, et cetera? Communicate with those who share the load and try to restore harmony.

King of Pentacles

Like the Queen of Pentacles, the King of Pentacles represents someone who is a faithful and dedicated provider of not only wealth but also family stability. This card can symbolize someone others turn to for advice; look for a person who is reliable and steady but can also make solid and well-informed financial decisions.

In reverse, the King of Pentacles can be a sign that we've become thriftless and irresponsible with finances and resources. This may be a person who is so preoccupied with their social status they make significant financial errors, leading to ruin for their family. This card suggests you should take a good hard look at your relationship with money and wealth. Ask yourself whether you are living with a mindset of abundance or of scarcity. Be cautious of those who would take advantage of your financial situation to achieve their own gains.

11
SIMPLE SPREADS

When you're reading Tarot for divination, the possibilities for spreads, or layouts, are virtually endless. Whether you're looking at cards for yourself or others, you'll soon find you connect better with some spreads than others–and that's okay! The spread is the pattern in which the cards are displayed, and each position is assigned a divinatory meaning. The cards in the various positions will guide you in your process as you evaluate their meanings and determine what potential outcomes lie ahead.

It's important to note that the layouts shared here are the ones I've used for decades because they work best for me. If you find you need to adjust and change these spreads, or the meanings of the cards in the various positions, do so! The key is to be consistent each time you read and not change meanings mid-reading to suit what you hope to see happen.

To begin each reading, start by shuffling your deck thoroughly. As you turn the cards over, place them in the order of the positions listed in the layout. If you have a specific question you'd like answered, think about it as you lay out the cards. You can also do a generalized reading to get a sense of what's presently going on by not focusing on a specific issue at hand. Often, the cards will answer the question you should have asked anyway rather than the one you did ask. Finally, it's up to you whether you turn all the cards over immediately, as you lay them down, or whether you flip them over one at a time as you read them. Use the method that makes the most sense to you.

THREE-CARD LAYOUT

If you're a beginner to Tarot—or someone who's been practicing for a while but wants a simple layout—try this three-card spread. Lay the three cards out from left to right, side by side. The first one is designated as Card 1 and represents past influences. The second one, Card 2, should be in the center, and it symbolizes the current situation. Finally, Card 3, the last one, shows potential future outcomes.

You may wish to modify this spread to suit your own needs by assigning different meanings to the three cards, such as Situation/Obstacle/Advice or Idea/Process/Results. If you'd like to alter it for a specific topic, you could change it to You/Partner/Relationship for love insight or Mind/Body/Spirit for a reading on well-being. In other words, any question with three parts can work with this layout.

CARD 1: PAST INFLUENCES

Simply saying the past can be a very vague concept, but in general, you can view the messages of this card as showing events, feelings, or people that impact what's currently taking place. Does it mean things that took place in years gone by, perhaps even in your childhood? Maybe . . . or it could be an event or conversation that happened just a few days ago. The past—no matter how long ago it was—is significant because everything you've done throughout your life informs the person you are now as well as the one you will later become. The influences of the past can be good or bad; the important part is to recognize that they have some bearing on where you are currently.

CARD 2: CURRENT SITUATION

The center card symbolizes the present, the important things surrounding you right now. Because this spread is a basic one with only three cards, many messages can be read into this center card that may normally be seen across several cards in a larger spread. This card could reveal how others view what's going on, external influences taking place, hidden obstacles you haven't yet uncovered, and so on.

CARD 3: POTENTIAL FUTURE OUTCOMES

Our last card represents the final outcome—but with a caveat. That outcome could change at any time; it's based upon where things stand now. This can represent a long-term goal or an immediate resolution depending on the question and the situation you face. The messages on the card in this position aren't necessarily etched in stone; if you don't like what a card is telling you, change your behaviors, and your long-range outcome will go in a different direction.

Five-Card Layout

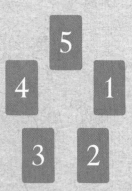

In many parts of the witchcraft community, the pentagram—a five-pointed star—is considered sacred, and this magical symbol has many different meanings. Within the star itself, each of the five points has a meaning; typically, they represent the four classical elements of earth, air, fire, and water. The top point is often assigned to Spirit, sometimes seen as a fifth element. This spread incorporates all five elements and their associated correspondences.

Lay the cards out in the five points of a star, beginning with the point on the upper right. This card represents the element of earth. Below it, on the lower right, place a card to symbolize the element of air. Working around the star, place a card to embody fire at the lower left, and on the upper left, lay down a card to represent water. Finally, at the very top point of your star, put down a card for the element of Spirit.

TOP CENTER—SPIRIT: THE WHOLE SELF

Finally, at the top center, is the card of Spirit. This card represents the whole self, the culmination of your journey, and the total of what all the other cards embody. Examine the previous four cards to see what they reveal not individually but as an entire message. How do they add up to present the sum of Spirit? How will things be resolved if you stay on your current path? What will be the end result of all the combined internal and external influences on your issue?

UPPER LEFT—WATER: THE TIDES OF INTUITION

The next card in this spread represents water, which is typically associated with wisdom and intuition. Ultimately, this is where you'll find what your intuition is telling you; this card often confirms what you already knew but may have been denying. What can you learn from this situation? Can you adapt your current circumstances to meet your future needs and goals?

UPPER RIGHT—EARTH: KEEPING GROUNDED

The element of earth is deeply tied to security and stability; it's the element that represents what grounds us and what keeps us from taking steps ahead. Is there something holding you in place or back? Are there circumstances that prevent you from moving forward? This card will help reveal what has made your situation stagnant or what will allow it to progress toward completion.

LOWER LEFT—FIRE: THE ULTIMATE DESTROYER

Moving over to the bottom left, the element of fire embodies strong will and energy. Fire is a source of creation and destruction, so this is an opportunity to ask if you are sabotaging your own goals. What sort of internal conflicts is influencing the situation? If you're experiencing self-doubt, misapprehension, or feelings of unworthiness, their root causes could appear in this card.

LOWER RIGHT—AIR: THE WINDS OF INFLUENCE

Traditionally, air is related to matters of inspiration and communication. This card signifies what other people are telling you. Is somebody in your life providing a positive influence or are they dragging you down with negative messages? What sort of external forces is influencing your life right now? Are you relying on information from other people or finding the inspiration to make your own decisions by being well-informed?

Seven-Card Layout

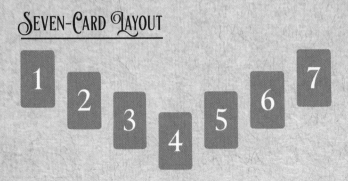

The seven-card layout–sometimes called a horseshoe spread–is one of the most popular spreads in use today. Various readers lay their horseshoes out differently–some with the open end down and others with the open end up. I like to lay mine out so the horseshoe curves like the letter U because that shape is associated with good fortune–and who doesn't want a bit of that? While some people see a horseshoe with the open end at the bottom as an invitation for good luck to drain out, in some folklore, this positioning makes the horseshoe a symbol of protection. Use the direction which appeals to you most.

For this layout, put down seven cards from left to right, in the shape of a horseshoe or U. The first card, Card 1, represents the past. Card 2 symbolizes the present, and Card 3 reveals hidden influences. The center card, at the curve of the U, is Card 4, and it indicates the querent, whether that be you if you or the person you are reading for. Card 5 is associated with the attitudes of other people involved in whatever is taking place, and Card 6 shows what you can do to solve the problem or move forward from the issue. Finally, Card 7, the last card, will display the likely eventual outcome of the situation.

CARD 1: THE PAST

This first card in the layout represents events from the past that have an influence on the current situation or question at hand. What elements of your previous experience—or events leading up to the present circumstances—are relevant?

CARD 2: THE PRESENT

The second card in the horseshoe spread reveals what's taking place in the present. What current events are circling around you and influencing the issue about which you are concerned?

CARD 3: HIDDEN INFLUENCES

This card is a little bit tricky because it represents the unseen; this is symbolic of problems and conflicts you don't yet know about. This card's information will only be revealed if you know to look for the right information. Could you be overlooking something important that's right under your nose, or is there something you simply refuse to acknowledge?

CARD 4: YOU

The fourth card in the spread, at the hump of the horseshoe, is you, sitting at the center of everything. Some people like to turn this card over first because it represents the self as well as your attitudes about the situation at hand. Is it a negative card, indicating you're concerned or fearful, or is it a positive, hopeful one, showing your optimism? Overall, this card will give you a good sense of what you really feel and think rather than what you've told others you feel or think.

CARD 5: THE INFLUENCE OF OTHERS

What sorts of external influences are dominating your situation? Do you accept help and support from other people in your life, or do you let other people drag you down? This card is important because it demonstrates how other people close to you feel about the situation—and rest assured, many of us are influenced by others' opinions.

CARD 6: WHAT SHOULD YOU DO?

The sixth card reveals the course of action you should take moving forward, and sometimes, what you should do is nothing at all. The situation could well be resolved if you follow this card's guidance.

CARD 7: THE FINAL OUTCOME

This last card factors in all six previous cards into its answer to provide to indicate a final resolution to the problem. Remember, if you don't like what you're seeing as the outcome, consider doing something different and changing your course.

Nine-Card Layout

A nine-card layout functions in a similar manner to the three-card spread on page 87 but allows us to get deeper insight into what's going on and how things are likely to go. By looking at a combined three cards each for the past, present, and future, we can see more complex meanings than we do with a single card in each spot.

This layout is sometimes referred to as a box spread because the nine cards are laid out in three rows of three, forming a square or rectangle. For this layout, pull your cards and lay them out in order from left to right forming three horizontal rows. Your top row will be Cards 1, 2, and 3; the middle is 4, 5, and 6; and cards 7, 8, and 9 run along the bottom.

Here's where this layout can get really interesting–although you've laid them out horizontally, you can start by reading them vertically in columns. Cards 1, 4, and 7 represent past influences–or whatever other meaning you've assigned them–and 2, 5, and 8 explain the present situation. Finally, the three cards on the end of each row–3, 6, and 9–are your potential future outcome.

Additionally, you can view the rows themselves as providers of extra insight. In the first row across, read Cards 1, 2, and 3 for a general overview of the situation at hand. The second row, Cards 4, 5, and 6, can show us an overall answer to the question. The last row, Cards 7, 8, and 9, can reveal hidden influences on the circumstances surrounding your problem.

12

READING INTUITIVELY

Once you've gotten the hang of laying out cards and interpreting
their meanings, it's time to step your Tarot game up a little bit.
Try challenging yourself to rely less on the traditional meanings—
the ones we discussed in part 2, or the explanations in your deck's
little book—and instead, allow yourself to read intuitively.

When we do intuitive readings, we trust our feelings about the cards' meanings and let them guide us without getting locked into specific definitions or symbolism. For instance, let's say you turn over a Six of Cups, a card historically associated with the idea that past events are impacting the present and future. However, when you look at it, that meaning just doesn't ring true—rather, for you, this card makes you feel like romance is burgeoning, with secret admirer declaring their previously unknown intentions. Does that mean the "past events" definition is somehow wrong for this card? Not at all, but what it does mean is that cards very often have different meanings for different people. By following your intuition when you read, you'll get a very different set of results than if you had followed the textbook definitions of the cards—and maybe, just maybe, that's what the universe wants you to know.

Although your mileage may vary, in my personal experience, when I started to trust my instinct was when I became really effective as a Tarot reader. You'll probably soon discover that the images in your deck—no matter which one you may be using—give you a very distinct intuitive feeling based upon the art on the card. I'd suggest you begin a Tarot journal of some sort to keep track of what you see and feel, recording your interpretations of your deck's cards for future use. Consider pulling a single card every day to get to know them individually; do this until you've written out a thoughtful analysis for each of the seventy-eight cards. Try some of these simple steps to begin understanding your deck intuitively.

Look at the card. This may seem like a no-brainer, but at first glance, what is the initial thought that pops into your head? Does it tell you a story with all the many pieces and parts combined, or do you have a basic, one-word impression of the card? This might be a good time to compare your initial interpretation of the card to its traditional meaning. Is it close, or does it seem completely unrelated? Is there anything in the standard definition that could be applied to your own assessment of the card?

Next, study the card and look for symbols or themes, which we'll discuss in more detail in chapter 15. Some of the best Tarot decks on the market today contain plenty of hidden information. Is there a particular icon or symbol that resonates with you or makes you feel a certain way? Does the card display a preponderance of a color that makes you happy, sad, or scared?

Think about your emotional reactions to the card as a whole. Do you have a sense of overwhelming joy or despair when you see it? What feelings do your life experiences bring to your reading of the card? Do you have family or ancestral traditions that inform your analysis of the card's meaning?

What story is the card's artwork telling you? Think about the people, animals, and environment in the imagery. Are the people—or other figures—in the image holding their hands in a certain way, displaying a specific facial expression, or carrying objects? What sort of clothing are they wearing, and does it reflect a particular social class or occupation?

You may find it helps to write down a description, such as *"There are two people wearing long robes at the base of a castle, and they're holding up bouquets of flowers—they look like they're happy! A bunch of other people* in the background looks like they're dancing and having a good time, and there's a lot of yellow, which is a color that makes me feel joy."

To take it a step further, once you've written your description down, think of the card as if you were in the scene yourself: *"I'm standing with someone I care about, we're holding flowers in the air, and all of our friends are celebrating with us. The sun is out, and I'm really happy."*

Ask yourself how the energy or feeling of the card relates to the situation at hand. Is there a connection? Can you peel the layers of the images and how they make you feel and see if there's a connection to what's currently taking place in your life? If you think deeply and mindfully about the card, it will give you more a personalized and unique insight on matters to come in the future.

Tarot Meditation

A quick note on meditation—first of all, no one has to meditate. Although many witches and other practitioners of magic do it as a matter of routine, there's no rule that says you absolutely must do so. However, you'll probably find meditating allows you to get into a magical headspace, and it's a lot easier to concentrate your attention on ritual, spellwork, or divination if you make meditation a regular habit. Keep in mind not everyone can meditate successfully the first time they do it. If you find yourself getting bored, restless, or unable to stay focused, don't worry! Just try it again another time. Like any skill set, it takes some practice.

To get to know your cards intuitively, start by doing this simple meditative exercise in which you'll pull a single card. Make sure you can sit quietly and undisturbed. If you share your home with others, consider waiting until they're out of the house, or ask them for a half an hour of peace and quiet while you're in the other room. Make a point to adjust your phone's settings so you won't get distracted by the pinging of notifications as you meditate.

If you'd like to play music as you meditate, do it! I'd recommend keeping the volume low so it's in the background. You may even want to try ambient tunes or nature sounds. Would you like to light a candle? Go ahead! How about some incense? Choose your favorite scent; some fragrances associated with the magic of intuition include frankincense, cedarwood, mugwort, or rosemary. Additionally, you'll need a pen and your Tarot journal or a notebook.

You should cleanse your cards before doing this meditation. See the card cleansing ritual in chapter 5.

Begin by sitting comfortably and holding your Tarot deck in your hands—don't lie down because it's easy to fall asleep once you get relaxed! Close your eyes, and breathe in and out, focusing on each inhalation and exhalation. Calm your body as you breathe, feeling the air flow into your lungs and back out again. As you inhale, visualize inspiration and energy entering you, making your body powerful and recharged.

Next, calm your mind. When you exhale, see the stress or distractions of your everyday life leaving, blowing away from you and into the universe. Imagine all of the things that keep you preoccupied flowing out of your mind like water, draining away so they can no longer bother you. This is your time to feel at peace. Breathe, relax, and simply be.

Select a card from your Tarot deck at random and open your eyes. Studying the card, ask yourself some of the questions from the previous section. What is the first word that occurs to you when you look at it? What symbols, signs, or colors jump out at you? How does it make you feel on a physical, emotional, and spiritual level?

Now, keeping your breathing regular and calm, visualize yourself inside the card. See yourself walking around the world that is portrayed in the artwork. Explore, following paths, observing people and animals, meandering amongst trees and buildings. Ask yourself—if you existed within that card, what advice would you give to someone looking in? What advice do you have for yourself based upon your surrounding environment?

How do you feel existing in the world of the card? Does it evoke negative, unpleasant, or even frightening emotions? Keep your breathing regular so you will remain calm and at peace. Know you are safe, and you are simply there to observe what's taking place around you. If the card makes you feel happy, content, and protected, that's a wonderful thing. Remember that feeling as well.

When you've achieved a deep understanding of the world you've experienced within the card, close your eyes once more, and allow yourself to return back to your position of comfort. Visualize yourself stepping out of the card, knowing you are once again in your safe, welcoming space at home. Take a few minutes to get yourself reoriented so you feel grounded and stable. When you're ready to open your eyes, do so with a renewed sense of energy, clarity, and knowledge.

Finally, with the card still in front of you, take your notebook and pen and write down everything you experienced as you traveled within the card. Make notes on the things you saw and felt—even heard, smelled, and tasted, if applicable. Be sure to include every detail; something that seems irrelevant or unimportant right now could turn out to have deep spiritual meaning to you in the future, so don't miss a thing. Once you've completed your notes, return the card to the deck. Later, when you need to refer to that card, you can go back to your journal and be reminded of the wisdom that was revealed to you.

13
CRAFTING A STORY

When you read Tarot, you may find it makes a lot more sense to view it as storytelling. By this, I mean imagine the cards as illustrating a novel and you, the querent, are the main character. Each card is like a chapter in the book and they don't make sense until you look at all of them in order.

By looking at your spread of cards as a whole rather than as individual parts, you'll be able to create a narrative that informs the magic of your reading. The more you do this, the more confident you'll become in interpreting your cards, leading you to a deeper understanding of what they have to say to you. I've found that for me, verbalizing the images and their meanings out loud is the most effective way to do this. If storytelling out loud isn't your thing, run through the story in your head instead, and it will work just as well. Whichever way you do it, see yourself as the omniscient narrator in your tale.

X - THE WHEEL

$\mathcal{A}$S YOU TELL YOUR STORY, TRY TO INCLUDE THESE ELEMENTS:

THE MAIN CHARACTER, OR PROTAGONIST: What do they look like? What are they experiencing? What events have led them to their current situation?

EXAMPLE: *This is a reading about someone who is facing a big decision regarding their relationship. Although things have been happy and positive for a long time, now it appears some stagnation taking place, and they're feeling unfulfilled. They have to choose what to do next.*

CHALLENGES: What's getting in the way and preventing the main character from moving forward?

EXAMPLE: *This person is facing a dilemma because while they know they aren't content, they feel obligated toward the people they're in relationships with. They fear if they leave, they'll be abandoning responsibilities or hurting people's feelings, which would make them feel guilty or in the wrong.*

OPPORTUNITIES: What potential opportunities or choices are available to your main character? What choices do they have that would allow them to move forward or resolve their situation?

EXAMPLE: *This person has a few different options. First, they could continue these relationships but find ways to make them more satisfying and rewarding. Another choice would be to put these relationships on the back burner, still maintaining them but at a less intense level. This would allow them to maintain the relationships' connections while investing more time in themselves than in the other people involved. A third option would be to end the relationships completely, understanding they've run their course, and walk away.*

THEMES AND SYMBOLS: What do you see most often? We'll dive deeper into this when we get to chapter 15, but watch for cases in which you see a high proportion of specific types of cards—Major Arcana, the suits, various symbols, etc.

EXAMPLE: *This spread contains a lot of Cup cards, which means relationships really are a priority for this person, but there are also several Swords appearing. That suggests a good deal of conflict going on right now as well.*

ENVIRONMENT AND ATMOSPHERE: in a novel, this would be your story's setting. What energy surrounds the spread? Is there much support from others for your main character's situation?

EXAMPLE: *This is an individual who has a strong support network. Family and friends always have their back, and they all have opinions on what this person should do. A few of them may have significant influence, but ultimately this person is going to do what's best for themselves in the long run.*

THE REWARD: What's the long-term payoff for your main character? In other words, what's their goal? Where do they see themselves standing once the situation is resolved?

EXAMPLE: *This person hopes to be content and happy once again instead of frustrated that they're doing all of the heavy lifting in their relationships. They'd like to see an equal division of the emotional labor rather than feeling as though all the responsibilities fall to them instead of shared fairly with the other people involved.*

THE OUTCOME: this is the final chapter for your protagonist. What does the future hold if things continue on their current trajectories?

EXAMPLE: *Ultimately, this person will make a decision that serves them well. They'll do what they need to relieve the emotional burdens they've been experiencing. Someone close to them will feel hurt by this, perhaps even betrayed, but in the long run, the person needs to prioritize their own needs over others' desires.*

Finally, ask yourself if your story is a satisfying one. How does it make you feel overall? Can you visualize yourself walking through the various chapters, navigating your way around potential obstacles and challenges, and ultimately being comfortable with the long-term outcome?

14

SHADOW ASPECTS AND REVERSALS

We all have parts of ourselves we don't want to examine. They're the parts we're embarrassed by and refuse to show the rest of the world, aspects of who we are that we find shameful or frightening. Acknowledging these traits, whether they are deeply buried or just lurking below the surface, can be difficult and complex. However, allowing ourselves to do so can be therapeutic and valuable because once we accept that those parts exist, we can cope with them in a healthy way. Working with our shadow selves can help us overcome the trauma of our past, move beyond harmful attitudes or behaviors, and shed destructive thoughts and actions that can cause pain in ourselves or those we love.

The concept of the shadow self was first introduced by Carl Jung, the noted Swiss psychiatrist, who posited that to be free of these aspects of our unconscious we suppress, we have to first understand what they are. Once we gain that understanding, we can integrate them into the way we see ourselves and push past the obstacles they have created for us. Although Jung's work is rooted in psychology, we can adapt it toward our spiritual development as well. In fact, Jung wrote in *The Archetypes and the Collective Unconscious*, "[It] seems as if the set of pictures in the Tarot cards were distantly descended from the archetypes of transformation . . ." (Carl Jung, *The Archetypes and the Collective Unconscious.*

With Tarot, we can use the cards' messages to take a deep dive into who we really are—warts and all—and chart a path forward to self-discovery and healing. For many people, working with cards that appear in reverse is a way to facilitate this journey. Remember when we discussed how Tarot card meanings appear on a spectrum? Nothing is black and white; everything exists in a liminal place, in between, and these reversed cards invite our shadow aspects to reveal themselves to us.

By working with reversed cards specifically, you can ask yourself—and ideally, find answers—to these questions:

* What do I need to heal, and how can I do it?
* What is broken that I need to repair, and how will it help me?
* What actions do I need to take to move forward?

Reversals

Many readers believe if a number of cards in a layout appear reversed, it could be telling you to pay attention to the shadow side of the spectrum when you evaluate the cards' energies and messages. This is one of the benefits of teaching yourself to read intuitively—a card's physical reversal represents what you are likely to understand through intuition. Again, it's important to remember that a reversed meaning isn't the exact opposite of what the message is when it appears upright.

Of note, not all readers read reversals. Some people find that since there are already seventy-eight cards in a Tarot deck, if they read intuitively, those seventy-eight cards should give them plenty of insight into their current situation. Adding reversals simply adds another seventy-eight meaning—for a total of 156 possible options!—that some readers feel is unnecessary. Whether you choose to read reversals is up to you, but be consistent. Don't read reversals only when they confirm your biases and then ignore them if the messages make you uncomfortable.

There are certainly downfalls to eliminating reversed cards from your readings. If the issue you're trying to sort through is complex or detailed, omitting reversals could leave out important insight, which means you're not really getting the full picture of the situation. On the other hand, if you're trying to resolve a relatively simple problem, you may find a spread with no reversed cards still manages to reveal everything you need to consider. As you learn to read intuitively, you'll be able to parse out the message behind each card and how it applies to you, whether it appears in reverse or upright. If there's a message for your shadow self, you'll see it no matter which direction the card is oriented.

Ritual to Work with the Shadow Self

This ritual involves a five-card layout, and I've found it a really useful way to get to the bottom of deeply buried issues. As always, I recommend keeping a notebook or journal handy, as well as a pen. Also, you may want to have a box of tissues on standby–shadow work can be profoundly emotional and may affect you in ways you didn't expect to experience. The cards you will be working with are:

* **CARD 1:** Your shadow trait

* **CARD 2:** Why you've kept it hidden

* **CARD 3:** The hard truth

* **CARD 4:** Potential benefits

* **CARD 5:** Self-care

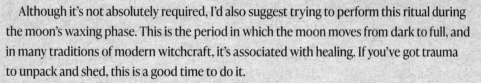

Although it's not absolutely required, I'd also suggest trying to perform this ritual during the moon's waxing phase. This is the period in which the moon moves from dark to full, and in many traditions of modern witchcraft, it's associated with healing. If you've got trauma to unpack and shed, this is a good time to do it.

In addition to your deck of Tarot cards, you'll need five indigo candles–a color associated with intuition, perception, and spiritual self-awareness. If you can't find indigo candles, white is a perfectly acceptable substitute.

1 Make sure you can work quietly and undisturbed. Hold your Tarot deck in your hands, and as you do, focus on identifying your shadow traits. You may not know what they are–after all, if you did, they probably wouldn't be shadow traits. If it helps you to call upon your spirit guides, guardians, deities, or ancestors for assistance, do so as you shuffle the cards. Once you've shuffled them completely, place your first card face down on your workspace. This card will reveal the shadow trait you need to work on healing. Place a candle beside it, and light it, saying *I call for illumination that I may identify a part of myself long hidden.* Turn the card over to see what it reveals. Take some time to evaluate what this card is trying to tell you, using probing questions to read it intuitively. Is this trait something you've wondered about before? How does it impact your current self-image and relationships with other people? If you need to write these thoughts down, do so, and then take a few moments to reflect on what the card has revealed to you. When you're ready, move on to the next card.

2 Place your next card, Card 2, face down behind the first one. This will reveal insight into why you've kept this particular shadow trait hidden. Light the next candle, and say, *I call for insight that I may understand why this part of me has remained in the shadows for so long.* When you turn the card over, once again reflect on the messages it contains. What is your intuition telling you about why you haven't shared this part of yourself with others or outwardly acknowledged it? Is it shame? Fear? Worry that you'll be perceived differently? What is it about this trait that has made you hold back? Write down your thoughts, reflect upon them, and then move on to Card 3.

3 Your third card, which represents the hard truth about your shadow trait, should be placed face down behind Card 2. Light another candle as you say, *I call for understanding that I may know the deepest truths about this shadow aspect of myself.* This could be the most emotionally challenging card in this layout. When you turn Card 3 over, ask yourself for deeper insight as to the foundation of this trait. Where does it come from? Could it be rooted in long-buried childhood trauma? Is it the result of some event—or series of them—that your unconscious self has repressed? Does it stem from your relationships with your parents or partners? What is the origin story for this part of you that has remained hidden for so long? Take time to reflect on this, writing your discoveries down. If you need to cry or scream, don't hold back; express whatever feelings you're having authentically. Once you've unpacked this and are ready to forge ahead, move on to the next card.

4 Place Card 4, symbolizing the potential benefits of this shadow trait, face down in front of Card 1. Light the fourth candle, and say, *I call for awareness that I may see the value in this part of my shadow self.* Flip the card over and take a deep dive into the positive here. There can be benefits found in our shadow traits despite origins that are often negative. Has this trait made you stronger and more resilient? Has it informed the way you cultivate and maintain relationships so you don't repeat a cycle from the past? Do you find yourself more determined and focused than ever to overcome what you've previously experienced? After some reflection, write this analysis down as well. When you're prepared to take the final step, lay down the fifth card.

5 Lay your fifth and final card face down in front of Card 4. This is the card of healing and self-care—how can you best move forward and heal yourself in a mindful way as you unpack the knowledge of your shadow trait? Light the candle, saying, *I call for knowledge that I may move forward from the shadows and heal myself in a loving way in the future.* Turn the card face up and see what it's telling you. What steps do you need to take to overcome the negative aspects of your shadow trait? How can you integrate the negative parts of this trait with the positive ones to create a happier, healthier, more balanced self? Which aspects of your life do you need to prioritize? Are there relationships— with yourself or other people—that you need to devote more time to repairing? Do you need to learn to set more stringent boundaries? Write down anything that comes to mind as you study the card in front of you.

When you're finished, take some time to regroup. Again, shadow work can be exhausting—mentally, emotionally, and physically. Find your calm; you now know what work must be done and have a richer awareness of why you need to do it. Once you're ready, extinguish the candles, and move forward with deliberate clarity.

15

THEMES TO LOOK FOR

The more you work with the Tarot, the more you'll begin to recognize specific themes. In particular, if you have a particular deck you prefer to work with all the time, you'll notice certain patterns emerging as you familiarize yourself with the cards. One of the benefits of understanding themes and patterns is they can draw a connection between two cards that otherwise may not seem to go together logically. By spotting these relationships between cards, you can gain a deeper insight into what's unfolding in your layout.

Multiples of Similar Cards

If your layout includes more than a few cards, odds are good you'll start seeing some cards that are related. For instance, you might lay out nine cards and discover that six of them are Cups, or that half the cards in your seven-card spread are from the Major Arcana. This could be a message that you need to pay attention to, but what could it mean? Keep these interpretations in mind when you see multiples of the following types of cards:

* **MAJOR ARCANA:** Many Major Arcana cards in a spread can be a sign of big spiritual changes and awakenings.

* **ACES:** A high proportion of Aces, or Ones, can indicate new beginnings play a valuable role in your layout.
* **TWOS:** A number of Twos can represent important choices and decisions are being—or need to be—made.
* **THREES:** Lots of Threes can be a harbinger of success and good fortune. Three is considered a magical number in many modern witchcraft traditions.
* **FOURS:** A preponderance of Fours may indicate satisfaction and contentment.

* **FIVES:** If you see a lot of Fives, it could be a sign of conflict and big changes on the horizon.
* **SIXES:** A grouping of Sixes is associated with positive omens and deep connections to others.
* **SEVENS:** When you see a lot of Sevens, look for possibilities and opportunities waiting to be manifested.

* **EIGHTS:** When your spread includes many Eights, watch out for repeating patterns; after all, an Eight on its side is an infinity symbol.
* **NINES:** Like Threes, Nines are considered a magical number. If you see a lot of them, it can emphasize the overall atmosphere of the suit itself, with Wands representing high energy, Cups connecting to relationships, Swords relating to conflict and challenges, and Pentacles pointing to material and financial needs.
* **TENS:** A large proportion of Tens can hint at movement toward completion.
* **COURT CARDS:** Watch out for a high number of Pages, Knights, Queens, and Kings. If you see a lot of them combined, it can be a sign that other people have a significant influence over the situation at hand.

Colors as Symbols

When you lay out a selection of Tarot cards, one of the first things that may pop out at you is the collection of bright, vibrant colors. Rider Waite Smith, in particular, is heavily illustrated with reds, yellows, and blues. If you're working with this deck or any other set that includes colors, think about the symbolic meanings behind the artist's color choices. The following meanings are based on traditional color associations, but you may find a particular color resonates with you differently.

 RED
Passion, energy, and strong emotions

 PURPLE
Intuition, psychic ability, and power

 ORANGE
Joy and creativity

 BROWN
Earthiness, stability, neutrality, and a connection to nature.

 PINK
Love, friendship, forgiveness, and compassion

BLACK
Protection and mystery

YELLOW
Spontaneity, happiness, and enthusiasm

WHITE
The higher self, inexperience, and a connection to the divine

 GREEN
Financial abundance, harmony, and envy

 GOLD
Divinity, spiritual leadership, and success

BLUE
Communication, wisdom, trust, and emotional and physical healing

 SILVER
Emotions, sensitivity, and empathy

ANIMALS AND OTHER IMAGES

In addition to the people who appear in your Tarot deck, you may spot animals or other symbols appearing regularly in the cards. Many of these have hidden metaphysical meanings, so if you see many cards in your spread featuring one or more of these items, think about what it could mean.

ANGELS OR WINGS: Messages from the divine

ANKHS: Immortality

BIRDS: Freedom, clear perspective, and long-range thought

BLINDFOLDS: Refusal to see what's there

CHILDREN: Hope and promise for the future

CITIES OR TOWNS: Society and community

CLOUDS: Revelations and ideas; dawning awareness

DOORS AND GATES: Transitions and change

FISH: Wisdom and knowledge; creativity

GRAPEVINES: Abundance, fertility, and blessings

HOUSES OR CASTLES: Security, safety, and family stability

INFINITY SYMBOLS: Ongoing effects of our actions

KEYS: Mysteries and hidden secrets

LILIES: Purity and innocence

LIONS: Strength, loyalty, and courage

PILLARS: Balance and stabilization

POMEGRANATES: Fertility, miracles, and power

ROPES OR CHAINS: Binding and restriction

SCALES: Balance, fairness, and justice

SPHINXES: Secrets, riddles, and the mysteries of life

TOOLS (HOES, HAMMERS, SCYTHES, ETC.): Hard work and accomplishment

WATER: Emotional health and well-being

WREATHS: Victory and success

16
Tarot Rituals and Spells

For many practicing witches, the question often arises of how to do spellwork or perform a ritual without spending a fortune on fancy, expensive supplies. If you're working on a budget, or you don't have access to a metaphysical shop when you need it the most, spellwork and ritual construction can be a challenge. You might find yourself just giving up and saying, *Well, I don't have the supplies, so I guess I'm not doing that spell after all.*

However, the key to being a truly effective practitioner of witchcraft is learning to think outside the box. After all, the idea of just bopping down to the local witchy store to buy some candles and a crystal is a pretty new one in the grand scheme of human existence. What did our ancestors do hundreds of years ago—or even a generation or two back? They worked with what they had. And if you've got a Tarot deck in your possession, you've got a whole lot of spell components readily available at your fingertips.

Spell components—herbs, candles, crystals, and so on—are symbols that stand in to represent a person, concept, or idea. If a candle can symbolize a concept, then a Tarot card with all of its images and associations can as well. Think about it—if you've got a deck of seventy-eight cards, that's a lot of symbols you can use. By working with a card whose symbolism aligns with your goal, you can craft a ritual or spell that performs as effectively as one using traditional magical components. With a bit of creativity and some effort, you can manifest your intentions using your cards.

Before doing any of these spells or rituals, do whatever work your magical tradition requires of you—casting a circle, cleansing your space, and so on.

Daily Decision-Maker Ritual

We all face choices daily, and often, the decision is an easy one—we know what we want or what's good and healthy, and so that's the route we take. But sometimes, we find ourselves facing a dilemma with two clearly opposing options, each with potential benefits and possible drawbacks. Some possible examples could be:

> **A.** I like where I live because my family lives in the same city, but there's no career potential here.
>
> **B.** I'm thinking about moving to a new town for a job, but I don't know anybody there.

A. I love staying home with my kids, but they're getting older so they need me less; maybe I should start my own business.

B. Opening my own business sounds terrifying; I could probably just wait a few more years until the kids have gone off to college.

A. My partner is a good person, but we haven't been happy for a while, and I'm considering ending the relationship.

B. I'd really like to repair my relationship, but I realize that it will take a lot of work and commitment; I'm not sure it's worth it.

So how do you choose between A and B if both have pros and cons to them? This ritual involves laying out Tarot cards in two clearly separate paths; while the cards can't make the decision for you, what they *can* do is give some insight as to which direction may be the right one to choose.

You can use this quick ritual each day if you face regular choices that must be made, or save it for when you have big decisions ahead of you. In addition to your cards, you'll need a pen and a piece of paper or page in your journal.

Before you even begin pulling cards, meditate on your dilemma. What are the two options you need to choose between? There must be obvious advantages and disadvantages to each. At the top of the paper, write your two choices (we'll call them A and B), and draw a line between them. You'll be pulling five cards for this ritual layout, all placed face down initially.

* **CARD 1:** Option A's advantages

* **CARD 2:** Option B's advantages

* **CARD 3:** Option A's disadvantages

* **CARD 4:** Option B's disadvantages

* **CARD 5:** Advice from the cards

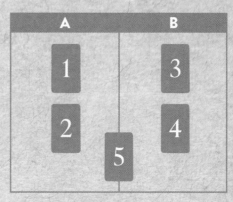

Lay them out so that Cards 1 and 3 are in the A column, and Cards 2 and 4 are in the B column. Finally, lay Card 5 at the bottom of the page so it overlaps into both the A and B columns.

1 Place your hand over Card 1, and close your eyes. Say, *Reveal to me the positives; reveal to me the benefits; reveal to me why this should be my choice.* Open your eyes and turn over the card. What messages does it have for you? What energy surrounds it? How does it make you feel–relieved, happy, excited? This card demonstrates all you have to gain should you select option A.

2 Repeat this action for Card 2 to show how you can expect to benefit if you choose option B.

3 Move to Card 3. Closing your eyes, place your hand over the card, and say, *Reveal to me the negatives; reveal to me the drawbacks; reveal to me why this should not be my choice.* Once you've opened your eyes, turn the card over and take a look. How does this card illuminating the negative repercussions of your decision make you feel? Are you frightened? Does it make you uneasy, angry, or sad? This card reveals the downsides of choosing option A.

4 Repeat this action for Card 4, which will reveal the negative sides of selecting choice B.

5 Finally, place your hand over Card 5, and close your eyes. Say, *Offer me advice offer me insight, offer me guidance, so I may choose the path that is best for me.* Turn the card over and see what it says. You may be surprised to see a clear decision ahead of you, favoring one option over the other. What words of guidance do you take away from this card to help you toward making your choice and acting upon it in a healthy and empowered way?

This spread can also be used if you have more than two options in front of you. If you have three or four choices, perform this ritual the same way by simply adding extra columns for choices C, D, and so on.

Tarot Self-Protection Spell

Let's face it, we live in a world where we often feel unsafe. Whether it's physical danger, emotional turmoil, or unhealthy relationships, there's always something from which we need protection. This simple spell is one you can do at any time, for any purpose—you don't need to use *all* of the cards outlined below, just the ones that apply for whatever your situation happens to be. Choose the card or cards that best fit your needs:

* **THE MAGICIAN:** gives you the power to manifest your intentions, even when others might be attempting to sabotage you.
* **THE HIGH PRIESTESS:** can offer protection and security against the unknown, including psychic or magical attacks.
* **THE EMPRESS:** provides loving, nurturing safety in an unstable family environment.
* **STRENGTH:** allows you to set protective boundaries and hold firm when others try to cross them.
* **JUSTICE:** affords protection in matters of legal battles.
* **THE DEVIL, REVERSED:** can help protect you and your loved ones from the burdens of addiction, mental illness, or obsessive behaviors.
* **THE WORLD:** offers protection against losing all the things you have worked for.
* **QUEEN OF CUPS:** can help protect you from the pain of a broken heart or other relationship issues, including emotional manipulation.

- ✴ **KING OF PENTACLES:** gives you the power to shield yourself from those who may be trying to take advantage of you financially.
- ✴ **QUEEN OF SWORDS:** can offer protection when you're facing known conflict with others.
- ✴ **KING OF WANDS:** can help protect you in your professional life, whether at work, school, or other collaborative endeavors.

In addition to the card or cards that aligns best with your current situation, you'll also need a hematite stone and a black candle. Try to do this working on either a Tuesday or a Saturday if possible; both of these days are associated with protection in many modern magical practices, as is the color black.

Place the hematite stone at the base of the candle. Light the candle, and hold your chosen card in your hands. Focus on the energies of the card and visualize the light from the candle flowing through you. Allow yourself to relax, calming yourself, and know you will be safe from whatever it is that is presenting a threat.

Say, *I call upon the powers of the [Name of Card], invoking your protective energies to watch over me, to envelop me, to keep me safe from harm. I banish all that would cause me pain; I banish those who might wish me ill; I banish all that does not serve my best interests or those of the people I love. [Name of Card], I call upon your protective powers to guide me and lead me forward in a way that does no harm to others but keeps me safe, happy, healthy, and whole.*

Pass the hematite stone through the candle's flame—be careful, don't burn your fingers! Say, *I send the energy of [Name of Card] to this stone—powerful, protective, and strong.*

Meditate on the protective properties of the hematite stone, and when you are ready, extinguish the candle. Carry the stone in your pocket as a talisman or wrap it in wire and wear it as a necklace. The stone will carry the protective vibrations of your chosen card and keep you safe wherever you go.

Spirit Guide Connection Ritual

Many people believe they have spirit guides, available to offer insight, wisdom, and direction when needed. But how do you find your spirit guide if they haven't revealed themselves to you yet? Sometimes, they simply haven't appeared because they don't know you're ready to listen, so one of the simplest ways to find yours is to do a Tarot ritual in which you call your spirit guide forward.

Whether you see your guides as guardians, protectors, or even angels, remember, their job is to *guide*; a spirit guide is not an entity you need to give your soul over to. Additionally, everyone's guides are a little different; yours might be an ascended master, an ancestral spirit, a teacher, or even an animal. Spirit guides can appear as representative archetypes; in other words, they can show up as someone who represents a concept or idea rather than an actual person. For example, maybe your spirit guide looks like Jane Austen. That doesn't mean Jane herself is your guide (although she certainly could be); instead, it may mean Austen represents certain things to you—wit, self-awareness, literacy, social commentary, and so on.

You'll need your Tarot deck for this ritual, which you should perform in a quiet place where you can work undisturbed. If you'd like to put some music on in the background or light your favorite meditative incense, do so before you begin. Seat yourself comfortably with your Tarot deck in your hands, and close your eyes. Regulate your breathing, inhaling and exhaling regularly. Clear your mind of anything that's not related to meeting your spirit guide; stop thinking about work, the kids, and that pile of dirty dishes in the sink.

When your mind is clear and you are fully relaxed, visualize yourself walking toward a closed door. It may take you a while to get to it—perhaps it is at the end of a corridor, or at the top of a mountain, or through a winding path in the forest. Take your time approaching it, enjoying all the scents and sounds of your walk. As you move closer, think about how the door makes you feel. Are you anxious? Excited and eager? Maybe a little frightened to see what's behind it?

What does your closed door look like? Visualize it clearly. Is it old and dilapidated, made of crumbling wood? Could it be large and metal, almost vault-like and full of secrets? Maybe it's brightly colored with runes or other magical symbols inscribed upon it.

Once you finally reach the door, pause for a moment. Think about what you hope to gain when you open it. You may even wish to speak aloud, saying something along the lines of, *As I open this door, I seek to gain the knowledge and wisdom of my spirit guide, or I open*

this door with an open heart, mind, and soul, ready to receive the messages that await me.
When you're ready, reach your hand out and open the door.

Behind the door, your spirit guide is waiting for you, and they have a message for you.
You might visualize your guide as a person, animal, or an archetypical concept. Know you're
safe in their presence; they are simply there to offer guidance and understanding. Now,
pull three cards from your deck. What insight do you see within them? What knowledge is
contained in the cards?

Take some time to think on the deeper meanings of each card individually, and then
explore the ways they all intertwine together to create the message your spirit guide wants

you to understand. What is your spirit guide trying to communicate to you?

How do you feel about the cards you've drawn? What emotions do they evoke? Are they cards of action, which will spur you on to make changes? Do they validate things you've long suspected? Do they reveal knowledge that was, up until now, hidden from you?

What is it about this message that's significant? Why is it important that you know it right now? Ask yourself these questions as you stand in the doorway, and if you need to, ask your guide. The answers may surprise you.

Take all the time you need to really evaluate everything that's been revealed. Be authentic with your emotions. Whether this message makes you angry or sad, happy or excited, or simply puzzled, your feelings are valid. When you are ready, thank your spirit guide for the wisdom they've shared. You may wish to speak the words aloud: *I thank you for the gift of this knowledge and appreciate the insight offered to me today.*

Visualize yourself closing the door and then walking along your long path home. On your return journey, again be sure to take in all in the environment around you—sights, smells, sounds. Keep your breathing regulated as you come back to your starting point and bring yourself out from your meditative state.

Be sure to write down the messages you received, particularly the specific cards you pulled, so that you can reflect on them in detail later on.

SWOT Tarot Ritual for Professional Growth

In the business world, there's a conceptual pl anning tool known as SWOT, which stands for Strengths, Weaknesses, Opportunities, and Threats. It's a great way to make decisions for project management and can help you gain insight on what's favorable about a situation and what areas need additional work. Like many aspects of business, SWOT translates very well into Tarot layouts. Although this ritual is designed to be used for professional growth and advancement—after all, consider SWOT's origins in organizational management—it can certainly be adapted for complex decision making and long-range planning in other areas of your life. By evaluating as many factors as possible, both those you can control and those you can't, you'll be able to gain a fresh perspective to solve your dilemma.

Before you begin, start thinking about an issue you're facing in your professional life. Some examples could be:

✳ I need to develop a stronger team, but we don't have the budget for it.
✳ I'd like to solve a recurring customer service problem, but we need more data.
✳ We're a small startup and we've been successful, but I need a clear picture of where we're going if we're ever going to grow.
✳ I'm up for a promotion, so I'd like to prove my worth by taking on additional responsibilities.

Write your problem down on a piece of paper, and draw a two-by-two grid below it, so you'll have four squares. In the top left, write the letter *S*. On the top right square, place a *W*. Below the S, on the lower left, write the letter *O*, and beside it in the bottom right, place a *T*. Shuffle your cards as you consider your situation.

This layout involves four cards (or groups of them), as follows:

✳ **STRENGTHS:** What kinds of things do you do well, whether you're naturally gifted at them or they are skills you've learned and developed over time? What do other people turn to you for help with? Where do your true talents lie?
✳ **WEAKNESSES:** Where do you fall short? What kinds of challenges do you regularly face? In what areas are you lacking resources or need to make improvements?
✳ **OPPORTUNITIES:** What can you take advantage of? Are there ways you can turn your strengths into opportunities? What doors are you ready and able to open using your existing skills and talents as a foundation?
✳ **THREATS:** Which things are presenting obstacles to you meeting your goals or achieving your dreams? Is there something or someone that can harm you? Do your weaknesses expose you to danger?

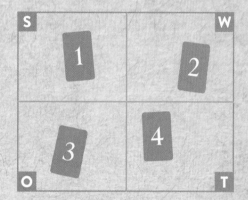

Place a card in each of the four squares. You may even want to put two or three in each spot for a richer, more insightful analysis. Look at the cards in each quadrant, exploring their deeper meanings.

As you look at your Strengths square, see how the talents identified in that section can be matched up with your Opportunities. How can you turn your talents into something that will benefit you and help you form an action plan to move forward? Are the Strengths aspects of yourself you can continue to develop?

Likewise, consider your Weaknesses square. Where are you lacking? How do these weaknesses impact potential threats? Are there improvements you can make to alleviate possible dangers? Are the Threat cards things you can leave behind you?

Look for all of the connections between the quadrants of this grid. Would eliminating some of your weaknesses open up more opportunities? Could your strengths be tapped into to help mitigate threats?

As you evaluate each square and its connection to the other three, try to tighten things up to outline a clear and attainable plan. For example, rather than saying, *Save my company money by working more efficiently,* you might say *Cut $100K in expenses by bringing in three new clients this quarter.* Be specific, be real, and be focused.

Once you've got concrete goals ahead of you, create a written action plan for solid professional change and growth.

17

MAJOR ARCANA CARD SPELLS

When it comes to spellwork and ritual relating to spiritual growth, intuition, and overall awareness of the self, the Major Arcana presents a perfect starting point. You can work with individual cards, based upon their meanings, to make all kinds of magic happen in your life.

Some ideas may include working with the Magician if you need decisive action that will help you take control of your own destiny. You might wish to use the Death card for spells involving a spiritual rebirth or a transformation of you who are and how you present yourself to the world. Bring out Strength for spells to give you courage, inner fortitude, or a spiritual pick-me-up. Call upon the Devil card for spells in which you banish toxic or harmful people, habits, or attitudes.

Try one of these spells for your magical workings with the Major Arcana.

CREATIVE MANIFESTATION

The High Priestess is a complex card full of mystery and wisdom. It's also associated with creative personalities, so it can be valuable to call upon the energy of the High Priestess if you need to manifest some creative power. If you're an artist who's stuck on a painting, a writer struggling with blocked words, or anyone else whose creativity has hit a wall, try this spell.

You'll need a yellow candle—a color associated with positivity and creativity—along with your High Priestess card. Try to do this working on a Wednesday if possible.

Find a quiet place to sit and light the candle. Holding the High Priestess in your hand, reflect upon the candle's flame. Feel its power, its energy, its magic. Consider all the ways you'd like to spark your creativity and what you must do to make your intentions into reality. Say, High Priestess, keeper of wisdom and knowledge, guardian of the powers of imagination, I call upon your energy to help me connect with the creativity of my higher self. I open my mind to new ideas; I open my hands to new skills; I open my heart to new endeavors. High Priestess, guide me to manifest all I wish to create.

When you're done, keep the candle and the card near where you create your art, and when you're ready to paint, write, or make again, thank the High Priestess.

HERMIT SPELL

GUIDANCE

The Hermit often reminds us there is wisdom out there waiting to be tapped, but we have to open ourselves up to the opportunity. In other words, you won't get the message unless you're willing to hear it in the first place. This is a card of guidance and self-evaluation and can be invoked when you need guidance in your decision-making process.

In addition to the Hermit card, you'll need a pendulum. If you don't have one, you can make a simple one by attaching a ring, key, or any other heavy item to a chain or string. You'll also need two pieces of plain white paper and a pen.

Place the Hermit in front of you at your workspace or altar. On each of the pieces of paper, write one of the choices you're facing. Hold the pendulum in your dominant hand over the papers, and feel your energy running through your fingertips into the chain or string.

Close your eyes, and say, Wisdom, guidance, knowledge. I call for these things as I make a choice. May I be guided for the higher good, filled with wisdom to make the correct decision, and blessed with the knowledge that I have done the right thing.

Open your eyes, hold the pendulum over one of the papers, and watch to see if it swings. Move it so it dangles above the other paper. Which of your two choices got the most movement from the pendulum? That is the option the Hermit's energy is directing you toward.

OVERCOME OBSTACLES

The Wheel of Fortune is always spinning, reminding us we can forge ahead and make our own destiny. However, reality can keep us in check. Sometimes, we face obstacles that seem insurmountable and threaten to hold us back.

For this working, you'll need your Wheel of Fortune card, a paper plate, a marker, and a pair of scissors. If possible, do this spell outdoors as the sun goes down. Find a quiet spot where you can work undisturbed.

Around the outer edge of the paper plate, use the marker to write down the obstacles that are preventing you from realizing your goals and dreams—things like anger, poor self-image, fear. Once you've done this, hold the Wheel of Fortune in your hand. Visualize the wheel turning, ever in motion. Rotate the plate slowly, seeing yourself in the center of the Wheel, surrounded by these obstacles. Now it's time to eliminate and replace them.

Using the scissors, cut away the words you've written, creating a new circle—a new Wheel—without these obstacles. Next, use your marker to write around the new edge, listing the things that can help you move ahead—courage, ambition, assertiveness, joy. Envision the Wheel picking up speed around you as you overcome your challenges and emerge victorious.

Take the obstacle words you cut away, tear them into tiny pieces, and bury or burn them. Keep the remaining plate of positive words in a place where you can see it any time you need a reminder of the Wheel of Fortune's energy.

JUSTICE SPELL

Court Cases

Got a court case coming up? The Justice card symbolizes the rule of law, representing fairness and accountability. When you're facing an upcoming legal matter, it doesn't hurt to do a bit of magic in addition to all your mundane actions like showing up on time and being polite to the judge.

You'll need the Justice card from your Tarot deck, a small cloth bag with a drawstring, and three dried black-eyed Susan flowers.

Place the Justice card on your workspace, and crush the dried flowers over it, sprinkling the plant material around the card. As you do, say, Fairness and favor come to me; I call for justice to win the day. May the judgment be just, the outcome ethical, and the result what I deserve.

Scoop the dried flower crumbles into the cloth bag and pull it tightly shut. When it's time to go to court, tuck the bag in your pocket to bring a fair and just decision your way.

MOON SPELL

Boost Your Intuition

The Moon card represents so many things—our latent psychic gifts, mysteries, hidden messages, and perception, just to name a few. This is a great card to work with if you want to boost your intuition, allowing you both clarity and the ability to trust your instincts.

For this working, you'll need the Moon card, a bowl of water, and a notebook. Do this spell outdoors on the night of the full moon if possible. If that's not feasible, try doing it on a Monday, the day of the week associated with lunar energy.

Hold the Moon card in your dominant hand. Look up, feeling the powerful pull of the moon above you. How does it make you feel? Think about the powerful intuition we all have within us, just waiting to be explored.

Gaze into the bowl, being sure to position it so the moon is reflected in the water. Watch the reflection, shimmering and shining on the surface, and consciously clear your mind of mundane matters. Continue observing the moon's reflection, and watch for patterns, shapes, or messages to appear in the water. As you visualize them, what's the first thing that comes to mind as the images change before you? Write down all the things you see and what you think they might mean to you. Don't worry about whether the patterns and images make sense right now.

When you're ready, pour the water out of the bowl onto the ground. Over the coming days, take some time to interpret what you saw and what it could mean. Be mindful of whether or not the things you saw and felt in the moonlight have come to pass.

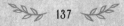

18

CUP CARD SPELLS

If you're planning to do magic connected to love, emotions, and family, Cup cards can be the perfect spell component.

For instance, consider the Two of Cups to represent a relationship you'd like to pursue with a person you hope to get to know better. Perhaps a Four of Cups will help you establish boundaries—and stick to them—in the context of a relationship you're already involved in. Try working with the Six of Cups to renew a relationship from the past. Pull out the Ten of Cups if the goal of your working is all about that happily-ever-after outcome.

Give one of these spells a try for your workings with the suit of Cups.

Ace: Initial Attraction

Aces appear at the beginning of each suit, so it makes sense to work with them in spells that call for new, fresh starts. The Ace of Cups is no exception, and it reminds us if we put effort into working hard to connect with others, we can enjoy rich and rewarding new relationships.

For this working, you'll need an Ace of Cups card, a small piece of red fabric, and a red ribbon. You'll also need dried basil and mint leaves. Try to do this spell during the waxing moon phase, as the moon grows toward full; this period is associated with attraction.

Seat yourself comfortably, holding the Ace of Cups in your hand, and meditate on the card as you visualize the virtues you wish to find in a relationship partner. Do you want someone who is a good listener? Physically affectionate? Likes to give gifts? Don't worry so much about the person's physical appearance—this is about the behaviors and mindsets you seek in a significant other.

Crumble the basil and mint between your fingertips, sprinkling it onto the fabric. As you do, inhale the fragrance of the herbs; these two plants are strongly associated with love. Say, *I draw love to myself, fresh and new. I draw attraction to myself, rewarding and true.* Use the ribbon to tie the piece of fabric shut with the basil and mint contained within. Carry this fabric pouch as you go about your daily routine; see who you encounter that fits your desired qualities in a partner. When you're not out around other people, keep the pouch safely beside the Ace of Cups in a place where you'll see it regularly.

CUP CARD SPELL

Three: Community Unity

The Three of Cups is a card of true celebration and joy—so why not work with it to bring about unity and victory within your community? You'll need your Three of Cups card, along with something to symbolize your community as a whole. This could be a flag, a business card, a piece of jewelry, or art—be creative and think about what represents your community best. Finally, you'll need a bottle or pot of your favorite beverage and three cups—yes, actual cups.

Place the Tarot card on your workspace with the symbol of your community before it. Take a few moments and reflect upon how far your community has come and what you hope to see it achieve in the future. Where do you want it to go? What steps need to be taken to bring people together for a common goal?

Pour some of the beverage into the first cup. Raise it up high, offering a toast to your community, and say, *I celebrate us, in all our wonder and joy, and wish for us unity and togetherness.* Take a sip from the cup. Add some of your beverage to the second cup, and raise a toast. Say, *I celebrate us, in all our power and strength, and wish for us influence and the bringing about of positive change*, and take a sip. Finally, pour the last of your beverage into the third cup. Raise it up, making your toast, saying, *I celebrate us, in all our similarities and our differences, and wish for us the power to unite, the power to influence, the power to change, and the power to stand together and make a mark.* Take your last sip.

When you are done, go start on the non-magical actions you need to take to bring about healing and unity in your group.

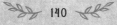

EIGHT: LOVE YOURSELF

If you feel like self-love has been lacking in your life, the Eight of Cups can help you refocus on self-care and healing so you can move forward from things that caused you to stagnate emotionally. By reprioritizing your own needs and well-being and allowing yourself the love you deserve, you can forge a healthier, happier connection to who you are.

You'll need your Eight of Cups card and rose quartz. Do this spell in the morning as you get ready to begin your day. Start by placing the Eight of Cups and the rose quartz next to your bathroom mirror, and then take a warm shower—but don't turn on the fan! Instead, allow your mirror to fog up with steam. When you're done showering, stand in front of the mirror and use your finger to draw a heart on the steamed glass. Wipe away the fog on the inside of the heart, so you can see your face clearly.

Hold the Tarot card in one hand and the quartz in the other, and begin speaking to yourself in the mirror. See the person you truly are, and congratulate yourself on all your good qualities. Say them out loud, as if you were speaking to a friend. As you speak, feel the positivity of these kind words flowing into the quartz crystal in your hand. Talk as long as you want! Give yourself the gift of patience, compassion, and love.

When you're done, get dressed, and start your day, carrying the rose quartz in your pocket. Leave the Eight of Cups near your mirror so you'll see it several times during the day, and be reminded of your loving words to yourself.

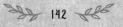

Queen: A Harmonious Relationship

The Queen of Cups is all about kindness, reliability, and understanding. It's a great card to use in magic related to keeping an existing relationship harmonious and balanced, without forcing one party to give more than they take simply to keep the peace.

For this spell, you'll need your Queen of Cups card, a light blue candle, a fire-safe dish, a piece of paper, and a pen. If possible, do this working on a Friday, which is associated with love, harmony, and reconciliation.

Place the Queen of Cups card on your workspace and inscribe the candle with your own name and the name of the person you're in a relationship with. Place the candle in front of the card and light it, taking a few moments to meditate as you watch the flame. Visualize the two of you, each compromising as needed to bring about greater understanding of each other in the relationship.

On the paper, write down words that describe any problem areas you've had in the relationship—things like *poor communication, jealousy, impatience*. It's time to shed those negative behaviors and emotions and move past them. Light the paper in the candle's flame, and say, *Harmony, balance, and healthy love, replace all the bad habits that damage us.* Drop the burning paper into the fire-safe dish and let it go up in smoke. Watch your bad habits be carried away in the ashes, and let the flame of harmony continue to burn for you and your person.

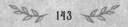

King: Find Your Home

The King of Cups is associated with the security and stability of a grounded home life—the place where your family is content. Thus, it can be a useful card for a spell designed to help you find the perfect home to live in. Remember, this doesn't always mean a big, fancy house—it is simply the place where you and your loved ones feel safe and happy.

You'll need the King of Cups card, a piece of nice stationery or paper, a pen, and an envelope. Aim for doing this spell on a Saturday, which is connected to the grounded energy of the land and home.

Keep the King of Cups sitting beside you as you search your local real estate listings—either homes for sale or for rent—and figure out what your ideal home is. What's within your budget? How many bedrooms do you need? Do you need a yard for the kids and dog, or are you perfectly content with a balcony? Do school districts matter to you?

When you find a home that meets all your criteria, print out a picture of it. Take your stationery and write a love letter to the home. Tell it why you and your family should live in a place just like this one.

Put the letter with the picture of the home inside the envelope, and seal it. Place the envelope beside the King of Cups in a place of honor in your current home, and be sure to acknowledge it each time you walk by.

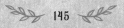

19
SWORD CARD SPELLS

The cards in the suit of Swords are typically associated with challenges and conflict, which can make them ideal for spells related to protection, courage, and confrontation.

If you're doing a working that is damaging or destructive, such as a binding or banishment, the Swords are incredibly valuable. You may wish to invoke a Three of Swords for spells related to pain and anger, particularly if there's been deception or a betrayal involved. Work with the Six of Swords to move past trauma and baggage from the past, or with the King of Swords for issues in which you need to assert your own authority.

Try one of these spells when you need the power of the Sword at your side.

Two: Protect Your Property

We all want to feel safe and know our belongings are secure from those who might cause mischief. When you're worried about vandals, thieves, or general disruption to your things, call upon the Two of Swords' defensive energy for a simple protection spell.

In addition to your Two of Swords, you'll need an item that represents the outside of your property—perhaps a bit of soil from the yard or a pebble from the parking lot. You'll also need a clear glass jar large enough to hold the Tarot card.

Place the card in the jar along with the soil or pebbles. Walk the perimeter of your property in a clockwise direction, holding the jar so the Two of Swords is facing outward toward any potential trespassers. As you walk around the property, focus on the protective energy of the card, and say, *This land is mine; those who would set foot here without permission are unwelcome. This home is mine; those who would enter to do me harm are unwelcome. These belongings are mine; those who would take them in thievery and deceit are unwelcome. Let only those with good intent cross this boundary.* Keep repeating this until you're back at your starting point.

Place the jar with the soil and the Two of Swords near your front door or window, keeping watch for troublemakers.

Four: Boost Your Fortitude

The Four of Swords serves to remind us that emotional and physical weariness can take its toll, and it's important to rejuvenate before we're completely wiped out. Use this working to rebuild your energy and your confidence, as well as your intestinal fortitude to tackle the conflicts ahead. Remember, if your low energy and exhaustion have medical or mental health origins, it's important to work with a health-care professional in addition to working magic.

For this spell, you'll need the Four of Swords card, four red tealight candles, and unscented oil. You'll also need powdered allspice, ground cinnamon, and a bowl for blending.

Set the card in front of you and meditate on its symbolism before you begin. When you're ready, place the candles on your workspace and light them. Red is a power color, one of strength. See the powerful, strong energy in the flames. Say, *I am brave, I am courageous, I am bold, and I am resilient.* Visualize your strength and energy returning to you, slowly at first and then building gradually as the flame grows and the wax begins to melt.

Add a few drops of the oil to the bowl, and then mix in the allspice and cinnamon to create a thick blend. Hold the bowl above the candle flame, and say, *Four swords bring strength; four blades bring bravery; four flames bring fortitude; four candles bring courage.* Dip your finger in the oil blend and use it to anoint your wrists and behind your ears. Store the rest in a container and anoint yourself whenever you need a pick-me-up or a boost of courage.

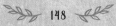

Seven: Silence a Liar

Want to stop a liar in their tracks? The Seven of Swords often indicates deception, so break it out for this spell when you know someone is telling lies about you.

In addition to the Seven of Swords card, you'll need a black candle, a piece of paper, a pen, and a pair of scissors. If you can, try to do this spell during the waning lunar phase, as the moon goes from full to dark; this period is associated with banishing and destructive magic.

Place the Tarot card in your workspace and light the candle. Focus on the flame for a moment and study the card. Think about the energy lies and deception bring into your life—it's time to banish it. Write the name of the person who's been lying about you backward on the paper; if you're not positive who it is, just write *Liar* or *Whoever speaks falsely of me.*

Using the scissors, slice the paper seven times, cutting through the person's name. As you do, think about the power of the suit of Swords. With each cut, say, *Seven swords, seven slices, your lies no more told. I banish you; I silence you; your words now grow cold.*

Burn the paper in the candle's flame. The liar's words will no longer have any impact upon your life, and eventually, they'll stop speaking about you altogether.

EIGHT: FIGHT YOUR FEARS

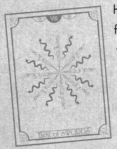

Have you ever been so afraid of failure that you couldn't move forward toward your goals? All the things you want to do—the things you need to do—are sitting by the wayside because you're scared. Being frightened is a natural part of human existence—change is scary—but when you're ready to finally take the plunge, try this spell to embrace your inner warrior and overcome those feelings that present obstacles.

You'll need the Eight of Swords for this and a sharp knife—or even a real sword if you can get your hands on one. If possible, do this spell outdoors, late at night when the moon is waning.

Go outside, holding the Eight in your non-dominant hand. Feel its energy. This is a card of conquering your enemy—your own anxieties, fears, and negative mindsets. It's time for you to shed your baggage and stop being afraid. Think about all of the things you'll be able to do if you can push past the fear—this is your moment to shine in battle.

Hold the knife or sword in your dominant hand and raise it to the sky. Speak softly at first, saying, *I am brave; I am strong; I am not afraid.* March around your yard, blade held high, repeating the chant, getting a bit louder each time. Scream it at the top of your lungs until you believe it—you are brave, you are strong, and you are no longer afraid.

When you're done yelling your bravery to the universe, it's time to acknowledge that you can face any challenges head on. When you do, you will be mighty.

Knight: Loyalty

The Knight of Swords is connected to loyalty, dedication, and strong convictions. If you're worried someone in your life—a friend, family member, or coworker—may be tempted to betray you, this spell can help facilitate their loyalty in the future.

For this working, you'll need the Knight of Swords card, a purple candle, and a piece of jewelry—a ring, bracelet, watch, or necklace—that you can give as a gift. You'll also need a length of purple ribbon. If possible, perform this spell on a Thursday, which is often associated with trust.

Inscribe the person's name on the candle and place it beside the Knight of Swords. Use the ribbon to tie the jewelry to the candle's base—it doesn't need to be snug or tight. Light the candle, and say, *We are tied together by trust; we are tied together by faithfulness; we are tied together by honor. I have earned your loyalty and will continue to deserve it from you.*

Allow the candle to burn out on its own. When it has burned away, untie the ribbon, and give the jewelry to the person whose loyalty you wish to retain.

20
WAND CARD SPELLS

If you're planning to do magic connected to jobs or career changes, education, or communication, consider working with the suit of Wands. This suit is perfect for matters related to your ambition and achievement, as well as issues tied to professional advancement. Associated with our thoughts and ideas, Wand cards can help connect us to the things that we're passionate about, as well as influence the way we interact with others in the context of our goals, hopes, and dreams.

You may choose to invoke the Three of Wands to represent hard work and collaborative efforts. Consider working with the Seven of Wands if you're concerned you could be outshined by people who don't always play by the rules. The Ten of Wands can be useful in spells relating to delegation and leadership. Think about calling in the Queen of Wands' energy for magical workings relating to kindness and compassion.

Ace: Ace a Job Interview

Do you have a job interview coming up? Congratulations! In addition to being fully prepared to answer questions, arriving on time, and dressing professionally, you can do a little bit of magic to improve your chances of landing the gig.

You'll need the Ace of Wands card, an orange candle, and unscented oil, such as grapeseed, olive, or sunflower oil. Before you head out for the interview, place the Tarot card at your workspace with the candle beside it. Light the candle, and as you watch the flame, visualize yourself walking self-assuredly into the interview and shaking hands with the hiring manager and other members of their team. Envision yourself being knowledgeable and assertive, impressing upon everyone that you are the right person for this role.

Dip your finger in the oil as you study the images on the Ace. Use the oil to trace a symbol upon your skin that represents the energy of the card. Perhaps you want to just draw a letter A, or a one, or some other sigil that is meaningful to you—maybe even the company's logo. Be sure to make this symbol in a place where it won't be noticed during your interview. As you mark it on your skin, see yourself happy and content at your new job.

Go to your interview, be confident, and knock it out of the park.

Two: Blossoming Business

The Two of Wands is associated with career and business advancement, particularly the type that stems from a growth in a new professional partnership. Did you recently start a new job or get a promotion with more responsibility? Are you considering some professional development so you can give your career path a clearer trajectory?

In addition to the Two of Wands card, you'll need a small flowerpot, some clean soil, a packet of seeds of your favorite flower or herb, and a permanent marker. Do this working during the waxing moon phase, as the moon moves toward full; this period is associated with attraction magic.

Place the flowerpot beside your Two of Wands and meditate on the card's energy. What images or messages come to mind? Using the marker, draw on the flowerpot, marking it with symbols you associate with success. Add the soil to the flowerpot, and then gently plant the seeds in the soil. As you do, say, *I plant the seeds of success, growing for the future. May these seeds blossom, bloom, and thrive, as does my career.*

Place the flowerpot in a sunny spot accompanied by the Two of Wands. Water it regularly, tending it with care, and as your seeds grow and bloom, your professional path will do the same.

Five: Clear The Air

The Five of Wands is deeply connected to discord and disagreements. If you want conflict to end, it means you will have to communicate effectively. You not only need to speak, but you also have to listen— and it can be hard to do both! However, clearing the air is the only way you'll be able to move past the disharmony. If you're the one in the wrong, own it.

For this spell, you'll need your favorite incense, the Five of Wands card, and a feather. Light the incense at your workspace and place it beside the Tarot card. Close your eyes, and take a few deep breaths. As you inhale the incense's fragrance, visualize the card's energy. This is a card of honesty and authenticity. It's time to be genuine.

Open your eyes, and gently fan the smoke from the incense with the feather. Watch as it drifts upward and dissipates. Say, *I own my errors; I own my mistakes; I ask forgiveness for where I went wrong. I accept that others make errors in judgment, I accept that others can be flawed, and I forgive those mistakes. The air is cleared, and we will begin anew, ready to speak, listen, and share.*

Allow the incense to burn out on its own, and then take any steps you need to move forward from the disagreement.

EIGHT: LEADERSHIP

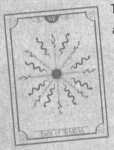

The Eight of Wands is a card of rapid movement and quick, decisive action—and this makes it ideal to use in spells related to leadership. Like other Eights, this one reflects ongoing, repetitive patterns; good leaders don't just do one effective thing and call it a day. Instead, being a strong leader requires a continuous action plan, lived daily.

In addition to the Eight of Wands, you'll need a pen and a piece of purple paper; purple is a power color associated with leadership and will. If you can, perform this spell on a Sunday, traditionally connected to matters of success and strength. Do it outside near a strong and sturdy tree.

Hold the Tarot card in your hand and study the card's energies. What emotions does it evoke? This is a card associated with advancement and enthusiasm. Are you excited about your leadership role? When you're ready, write the traits you associate with an effective leader on the paper; you may choose *fairness, integrity, wisdom, patience*. Cover the entire piece of paper with leadership words, and then fold it three times.

Find a nook or crevice in the tree and tuck the paper inside. Say, *I will strive to lead by listening, to guide others with my words, and to set examples by my actions. I will hear criticisms and be inspired to do better, I will mentor others to lead as well, and I will be the leader others wish to see in me. I will be strong; I will be sturdy; I will be dependable.*

Take a few more minutes to reflect upon the Eight of Wands' energy. Check to make sure your paper is securely hidden in the tree, and then walk away without looking back.

King: Confident Communicator

The King of Wands represents a true leader. This is the sort of person who got where they are by being genuine, friendly, and inspirational. It's the perfect card to work with if you want to influence others in an authentically positive way. By becoming a confident communicator, you'll be able to persuade people to see your point of view and to work with you toward achieving your vision.

In addition to the King of Wands card, you'll need a gemstone associated with communication and the throat chakra, such as lapis lazuli, turquoise, or aquamarine. Try to do this spell on a Wednesday—it's a day associated with confidence and influential speech.

Place the King of Wands in front of you, and close your eyes, holding the gemstone between your hands and sensing its cool surface in your palms. Run your fingers over the stone—how does it feel? Is it smooth or rough? Does it have rounded edges or jagged ones? Hold the stone before you, and then move it close to your throat and mouth. Visualize the assertive, encouraging King of Wands energy flowing through the stone. Say, *My voice is strong and self-assured; my voice is authentic and inspiring; my voice is confident and clear.*

Keep the stone in your pocket or some other place where you can readily access it. When it's time to speak up, run your fingers over the surface of the gemstone, being reminded of the confidence the King of Wands inspires.

21
PENTACLE/COIN CARD SPELLS

When it comes to the material aspects of your life, like money, investments, security, and stability, Pentacle cards are the perfect place to start.

\Work with the Two of Pentacles for magic to help you get your budget under control or to eliminate debt. Consider calling on the Seven of Pentacles for a spell in which you manifest the long-term benefits of all your hard work. Use an Eight of Pentacles to represent a promotion, raise, or recognition at work. For workings related to education—including paying tuition and obtaining financial aid—break out the Page of Pentacles.

Give your prosperity magic a boost with these spells invoking the Pentacle cards.

PENTACLE SPELL

Ace: Bank Account Abundance Magic

Aces are all about beginnings, and if you've ever needed to begin saving up for a rainy day, the Ace of Pentacles is a fantastic component to include in your spellwork. In addition to following mundane guidelines like not overspending or avoiding additional debt, start building your nest egg with this simple working.

You'll need the Ace of Pentacles and a blank check; if you don't own a checkbook, don't worry; you can draw one on a piece of paper or create one on your printer. Start by writing out a check to yourself—what dollar amount would be a good beginning point to kick-start your savings plan?

Keep it realistic; we'd all love to have a million bucks land in our checking account, but that's not likely to happen. Would $100 be enough to motivate you toward saving for the future? How about $50? Pick the number that inspires you and write the check for this amount.

On the line for the date, write *The future*, and at the signature line on the bottom, sign *The universe*. Wrap the check around the Ace of Pentacles card, and say, *New beginnings to come; new starts abound; new savings underway; new fortunes found.*

Tuck the Ace wrapped in the check safely away in a place you associate with money—your wallet, purse, or even the desk where you sit to pay bills each month. Be mindful of potential opportunities in the next few weeks to increase your financial growth.

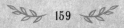

Three: Teamwork Makes The Dream Work

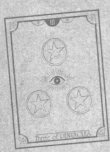

The Three of Pentacles is a card of strong collaborative energy, so if you were the kid who did all the work in your high school group project while others took the credit, this card has your back. Work with the Three of Pentacles when you want to strengthen the bond between a group of people working together toward a common goal.

For this working, you'll need a Three of Pentacles card, a yellow candle, and rose oil. You'll also need a piece of paper and a pen. Try to perform this spell on a Friday, a day on which alliances are traditionally forged.

Place the Tarot card in your workspace and inscribe the candle with a word or image that represents teamwork to you. You may try a single word like *collaboration* or *cooperation*, or you can create a symbol of your own. Light the candle, and as it burns, consider the Three of Pentacles' energy. How can you influence your group to collaborate for a shared, positive outcome?

On the paper, write down the names of each team member, then write down their strengths and skills. You might put Tina: *super tech skills*, Kwame: *amazing with number crunching*, and Chris: *creative problem-solver*. Dab a bit of the rose oil on your finger and use it to circle each person's name. As you do, speak their name aloud, and express your appreciation for their

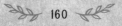

skill set and talents. *Kwame, I love working with you because I know you're going to keep us on task and under budget. Tina, your tech skills are unparalleled and I'm so glad you're working on this project.*

Once you've circled all of your team members, continue using the rose oil to draw lines connecting each of them to all of the other people in the group. Every circle should be joined to all of the other circles equally. While you're connecting them, say, *Working together, joined together, collaborating together, all for the common good.*

When everyone is joined together, fold the paper three times, tuck it under your burning candle, and leave it alone. Let the candle burn out on its own.

PENTACLE SPELL

Six: For Gratitude

When it comes to generosity and gratitude, the Six of Pentacles is a perfect card to use for magic. It reminds us that charitable giving is important but being thankful enough to count our blessings has considerable value as well.

For this spell, in addition to having your Six of Pentacles on hand, you'll need a pink candle; pink is a color associated with gratitude. If you can, perform this working at sundown. Before you begin, cook your favorite meal, and pour a glass of your favorite beverage.

Set yourself a place at your dining table, and light the candle, placing the Six of Pentacles at its base. Begin your meal, and as you take each bite, reflect on the things you appreciate in your life. You can speak them aloud if you wish—*I am so thankful I am healthy; I'm grateful I have a warm meal to eat; I am fortunate to have a family who loves me, et cetera.*

Each time you take a sip of your beverage, raise a toast to the Six of Pentacles, and say, *I offer thanks!* When you finish your meal and your drink, take a few minutes to reflect further on how fortunate you are. Say, *I welcome abundance into my life, and open myself up to even more things for which I can be thankful.*

Place the Six of Pentacles in a place where it can regularly remind you of the blessings you have in your life.

Ten: Prosperity

The Ten of Pentacles is, like other Tens, a symbol of completion. It celebrates our successes and achievements in all their many forms, and it is a card associated with family and stability. These attributes make it well-qualified for magic related to long-term prosperity, security, and abundance.

To do this simple working, you'll need a Ten of Pentacles, a green candle, and ten shiny new coins minted during the current calendar year. The ten coins should be pairs of different denominations of the currency you are using. For example, if you are using American coins, use two pennies, two nickels, two dimes, and two quarters—as well as a fifty-cent piece or a dollar coin. If possible, do this working on a Thursday, which is typically auspicious for money magic.

Inscribe a currency sign on the candle (use the symbol of the type of currency that is applicable to you—dollar, pound, euro, etc.), and light it, placing it beside your Ten of Pentacles. Surround the candle and the card with the coins one at a time. As you set them in place, count them out to enumerate your abundances like so: *One coin for hard-earned bounty, two coins for good fortune, three coins for finding luck, four coins for having plenty, five coins for achieving prosperity, six coins for appreciating blessings, seven coins for a stable home, eight coins for a secure family, nine coins for sharing joy, and ten coins for celebrating success with a grateful heart and a generous spirit.*

Allow the candle to burn out on its own. Once it has, gather the ten coins, and keep them in a special place, such as on your altar, to remind you of the abundance your life deserves.

King: Money Mindset

Do you live with a mindset of abundance or scarcity? Changing your outlook can significantly impact your relationship with your finances. By viewing yourself as prosperous instead of wanting, you can welcome prosperity into your life.

For this working, you'll need the King of Pentacles, modeling clay, and nine kernels of corn; grains symbolize the bounty of the harvest.

Place the King of Pentacles in your workspace and reflect on the card's energy. It's a card of wealth, long-term stability, and solid financial acumen. Is that the kind of energy you wish would surround you? Begin shaping the clay in your hands, pressing it together and molding it beneath your fingertips. Form it into a small bowl. As you do, visualize your hands drawing in money, welcoming it, and shaping it into abundance and plenty for the future. Say, *I draw in money; I draw in wealth; I draw in prosperity. I am blessed; I am stable; I am secure.*

In the bottom of the bowl, inscribe a pentacle shape—it doesn't have to be fancy, just a simple star within a circle. Place the corn kernels in the bowl, and say, *Abundance, growth, and blessings will always be before me.*

Keep the bowl in a safe place so it can remind you that you're not wanting, but you live a life of prosperity and comfort instead.

22

A Final Word

The Tarot—seventy-eight cards in the key of life, full of mystery and magic, insight and inspiration. As you move through your journey with these cards—no matter which deck you've selected for use— you'll find your world constantly enriched. You'll unearth secrets about yourself that have been long buried, you'll discover ways to move ahead with goals and plans for the future, and you'll develop a deep and rich understanding of the world and your place within it.

As you cultivate a stronger connection with your cards, you'll soon discover there's more to them than simply using them to see what's next. Study them, learn their energies, and understand the complexities behind each of these powerful little pieces of art. Understand your intuition and the knowledge you gain, and then transform that wisdom into proactive magic, ritual, and spellwork, tapping into the cards' energies.